The
Joy of Advent

Journey with the People, Events and Prayers
at the First Coming of Jesus Christ

Study Guide & Journal

Ten Studies

KAREN L. DWYER, PHD
and
LAWRENCE A. DWYER, JD

The Joy of Advent

Journey with the People, Events and Prayers
at the First Coming of Jesus Christ
Study Guide & Journal

Copyright © 2021
Karen L. Dwyer and Lawrence A. Dwyer
Heart of Jesus Publishing, Inc., Omaha, Nebraska

ISBN: 978-1-7367333-0-1

Printings: 2005, 2008, 2021
From Manger to Mission (2008)
The Advent of Jesus Christ in Holy Scripture (original title)
Nihil Obstat: Reverend Michael F. Gutgsell, Censor Librorum
Imprimatur: Most Reverend Elden Curtiss, Archbishop of Omaha
December 13, 2005, Omaha, NE
The *nihil obstat* and *imprimatur* are official declarations that a book is
free of doctrinal or moral error.

Cover Picture. *The Holy Night,* by Antonia da Correggio *(1530) Gemäldegalerie, Dresden, Germany.* United States Public Domain. The painting depicts Luke 2: 8-20 with the dazzling light radiating from the manger as Blessed Mary gazes at her newborn Jesus. Visible in the background is St. Joseph taking care of the animals and in the foreground, are the shepherds worshipping after coming in haste from the fields. [1]

DEDICATION

To our precious friends in the

Heart of Jesus Prayer Group
and
Martin's Bible Study

Table of Contents

Welcome to The Joy of Advent

The time of ADVENT, culminating in the birth of our Lord and Savior Jesus Christ, is a time familiar to most of us, but seldom do we take the time to linger over these passages in Scripture. That is the goal of this book. So, please join this joyful journey of faith and invite Jesus to speak to you in new ways as you meet the people, prayers, and events so important to His first coming. In this ten-part journey, you will meet Zechariah, Elizabeth, Blessed Virgin Mary, Joseph, John the Baptist, the Angels, the Shepherds, Simeon, Anna and the Magi, as you travel with them and partake in the most meaningful events in their lives.

You will discover three pairs of events related to Jesus' coming, including two annunciations, two births and two circumcisions. You will pray the four great prayers or canticles of the Church, including, Mary's *Magnificat* (Luke 1: 46-55), Zechariah's *Benedictus* (Luke 1:67-79), the Angels' *Gloria* (Luke 2:14) and Simeon's *Nunc Dimittis* (Luke 2:29-32). This journey that will take you back 2000 years ago to some amazing places. Through the Word of God, Jesus wants you to meet His family and friends and the Holy Spirit will be your guide.

The Format

This study is written in a format that follows St Augustine's guidelines for studying Scripture:

1. Read Scripture in its historical and cultural context,

2. Study the meaning of words in the original languages of Scripture (Hebrew and Greek), and

3. Apply basic truths and precepts to daily living.

Within This Study You Will Find

Connections. Each chapter starts with a Connection to help you prayerfully read the verses, reflect on the meaning, and connect the events of your life with the events of that time.

The Scriptures. Each chapter in this study contains the actual Scripture passages of the Luke 1-2 and Matthew 1-2 from the New Revised Standard Version-Catholic Edition (NRSVCE), approved by the United States Conference of Catholic Bishops and used with permission from the National Council of the Churches of Christ in the United States of America, or from the New American Bible Revised Edition excerpts from the Lectionary for Mass for Use in the Dioceses of the United States of America, second typical edition, used with permission.

Chapter Questions. Chapter Questions follow the *Connections*. The questions are grouped by themes to help you focus on the verses, follow the events and reflect on their significance.

Notes & Definitions. Historical notes offer background information. Definitions help explain the meaning of words in Scripture that may not be familiar to you today.

Commentary. Commentary among the questions provides cultural context, perspective, themes and summaries.

Application & Prayer Response. Each chapter ends with personal *Reflection, Application* and a *Personal Prayer Response* to help you apply the Scriptures personally and prayerfully.

Small Group Study. This study can be used for personal study and journaling as well as for small groups. See the Appendix for information on how to facilitate a small group study using this book.

1

Two Annunciations After 430 Years of Silence

Connection Question

What does Advent mean to You?

The Angel Appears to Zacharias in the Temple[2]
Painting by Domenico Ghirlandaio, 1449-1494
Public Domain

Chapter One –Two Annunciations

After 430 Years of Silence, Zechariah Meets Gabriel

The historical backdrop for the birth of Jesus Christ begins 25 centuries ago. This was the last time the people of God, as recorded in the Old Testament, heard God. The Lord had been silent for nearly 430 years. Not a word to His people who were anxiously awaiting the coming of the Messiah. This silence was unusual because throughout the Old Testament history, God would speak regularly to His people via the prophets. Hearing from God was important to the Israelites.

When we hear the word "Advent," most of us think that it refers to the four-week season that precedes Christmas and focuses on the anticipation of the birth of Jesus Christ. It does! In addition, Advent is meant to focus our attention on the present coming of Jesus in our own lives, as well as on the second coming of Jesus at the end of the world (Acts 1: 11) when he will bring a new heaven and a new earth (Revelation 21, 2 Peter 3: 11-13) and we will reign with him forever (2 Timothy 2: 11-13).

The word Advent comes from the Latin word "adventus" which means "coming." In New Testament Greek, "Parousia" is translated "coming" and it often refers to Christ's second coming. Of course, we cannot eagerly await the second coming of Jesus Christ unless we fully understand his first coming. So, the time of Advent opens many opportunities for us to experience hope and joy as we look forward to both comings, seeking to draw very close to Jesus.

In Chapter ONE of our study, we start with the Old Testament books of Hosea and Zechariah to learn why God would suddenly go silent. Next, we move to Luke 1 to hear two important annunciations after the 430 years of silence. The term "annunciation" in Latin means announcement. So, God began speaking again, and He sent announcements through His most important heavenly messenger.

Likely, you have heard of the annunciation made by the angel Gabriel to Blessed Mary proclaiming the birth of Jesus Christ. This announcement is often simply called "The Annunciation." In most dictionaries, the definition of annunciation is this: "The church festival in commemoration of the announcement of the Incarnation to the Virgin Mary that occurs on March 25th every year."[3] But there is another important annunciation preceding the one to Mary. It is the announcement Gabriel made to Zechariah, declaring the birth of

John the Baptist, the forerunner of Christ, the one who would come in the spirit and power of Elijah…to prepare a people fit for the Lord" (Luke 1:17).

To the people of the Old Testament, Gabriel's appearance and his message was startling. Why? God had stopped speaking for a long time and now He was speaking again. The silence was over. That is where the first part of our journey leads us.

Chapter One Questions

1. GOD STOPS SPEAKING.   Read Zechariah 7: 9-12 and Hosea 11: 1-4. (a) Circle the verses that indicate why God could be displeased with His people and stop speaking to them. (b) According to Hosea 11: 3-4, what had the people of God forgotten? (c) What similarities do you note between the people described in Zechariah or Hosea and those living in our culture today?

_____
_____
_____
_____
_____
_____

Zechariah 7: 9 – 12 (about 520 BC). The word of the Lord came to Zechariah, saying: Thus says the Lord of hosts: Render true judgments, show kindness and mercy to one another; 10 do not oppress the widow, the orphan, the alien, or the poor; and do not devise evil in your hearts against one another. 11 But they refused to listen, and turned a stubborn shoulder, and stopped their ears in order not to hear. 12 They made their hearts adamant in order not to hear the law and the words that the Lord of hosts had sent by his spirit through the former prophets. NRSVCE

Hosea 11: 1 – 4 (about 750 - 722 BC). When Israel was a child, I loved him, and out of Egypt I called my son. 2 The more I called them, the more I went from me; they kept sacrificing to the Baals and offering incense to idols. 3 Yet it was I who taught Ephraim to walk, I took them up in my arms; but they did not know that I healed them. 4 I led them with cords of human kindness, with bands of love. I was to them like those who lift infants to their cheeks. I bent down to them and fed them. NRSVCE

God Stopped Speaking, But He Left a Promise

God stopped speaking to His people because they stopped listening to Him. They stopped doing His will. They hardened their hearts. They refused to follow God and His commandments.

God always gives His people free will, and in this case, the people chose NOT to listen. Even in silence God was communicating to them. In Malachi 4: 5-6, written about 430 BC, God promised to send a Messiah and a forerunner:

Lo, I will send you the prophet Elijah before the great and terrible day of the Lord comes. He will turn the hearts of parents to their children and the hearts of children to their parents..." NRSVCE

Then, in Luke 1: 17 we read of the fulfillment of God's promises in Malachi — His plan to send His Son Jesus Christ and the forerunner John the Baptist, in the style of the great prophet Elijah:

"With the spirit and power of Elijah he will go before him, to turn the hearts of parents to their children, and the disobedient to the wisdom of the righteous, to make ready a people prepared for the Lord." NRSVCE

Now, we understand the backdrop of the coming of Jesus Christ — the people had fallen away from God. They had stopped listening to Him, worshipping Him and obeying Him. They turned to idols and even sacrificed babies to them. God warned the people, so when they stopped listening, He stopped speaking. Next in Luke 1, we meet the Angel Gabriel. He appears to Zechariah while praying and offering incense in the temple. Zechariah is the first person recorded in Scripture to hear from God almost 430 years after the prophet Malachi wrote the last book of the Old Testament.

2. *LUKE 1: 1-25.* (a) Please read Luke 1: 1-25 below and <u>CIRCLE</u> what catches your attention. (b) What does v. 5 indicate about the historical time period?

_____

_____

_____

_____

Luke 1: 1-25

Since many have undertaken to set down an orderly account of the events that have been fulfilled among us, ² just as they were handed on to us by those who from the beginning were eyewitnesses and servants of the word, ³ I too decided, after investigating everything carefully from the very first, to write an orderly account for you, most excellent Theophilus, ⁴ so that you may know the truth concerning the things about which you have been instructed. ⁵ In the days of King Herod of Judea, there was a priest named Zechariah, who belonged to the priestly order of Abijah. His wife was a descendant of Aaron, and her name was Elizabeth. ⁶ Both of them were righteous before God, living blamelessly according to all the commandments and regulations of the Lord. ⁷ But they had no children, because Elizabeth was barren, and both were getting on in years.

⁸Once when he was serving as priest before God and his section was on duty, ⁹ he was chosen by lot, according to the custom of the priesthood, to enter the sanctuary of the Lord and offer incense. ¹⁰ Now at the time of the incense offering, the whole assembly of the people was praying outside. ¹¹ Then there appeared to him an angel of the Lord, standing at the right side of the altar of incense. ¹² When Zechariah saw him, he was terrified; and fear overwhelmed him. ¹³ But the angel said to him, "Do not be afraid, Zechariah, for your prayer has been heard. Your wife Elizabeth will bear you a son, and you will name him John. ¹⁴ You will have joy and gladness, and many will rejoice at his birth, ¹⁵ for he will be great in the sight of the Lord. He must never drink wine or strong drink; even before his birth he will be filled with the Holy Spirit. ¹⁶ He will turn many of the people of Israel to the Lord their God. ¹⁷ With the spirit and power of Elijah he will go before him, to turn the hearts of parents to their children, and the disobedient to the wisdom of the righteous, to make ready a people prepared for the Lord."

18 Zechariah said to the angel, "How will I know that this is so? For I am an old man, and my wife is getting on in years." 19 The angel replied, "I am Gabriel. I stand in the presence of God, and I have been sent to speak to you and to bring you this good news. 20 But now, because you did not believe my words, which will be fulfilled in their time, you will become mute, unable to speak, until the day these things occur."

21Meanwhile the people were waiting for Zechariah and wondered at his delay in the sanctuary. 22 When he did come out, he could not speak to them, and they realized that he had seen a vision in the sanctuary. He kept motioning to them and remained unable to speak. 23 When his time of service was ended, he went to his home.

24After those days his wife Elizabeth conceived, and for five months she remained in seclusion. She said, 25 "This is what the Lord has done for me when he looked favorably on me and took away the disgrace I have endured among my people." NRSVCE

Notes: Luke writes to "Theophilus" (v. 3) to give an orderly account of the life of Jesus Christ, based on eyewitnesses and "servants of the Word" (v. 2). "Theophilus" in New Testament Greek means "friend of God" or "one who loves God." Thus, we can conclude the Holy Spirit used Luke to write these words to us, "who love God" to give us an account of the life of Jesus.

"In the days of King Herod of Judea" tells us the historical context by referencing *Herod the Great,* King of Judea, who ruled in Jerusalem from 37 BC until his death in 4 BC. King Herod, a Jewish convert, built pagan temples and put a pagan symbol of an eagle over the Jerusalem temple. Herod's name in Greek means "descendant of heroes," which fits his huge ambition for power and magnificence.[4] Unfortunately, he will be remembered not as a hero, but as the ruthless, evil ruler, responsible for killing all the male infants in an attempt to kill Baby Jesus.

3. _ZECHARIAH AND ELIZABETH._ In the following space, record all the facts you find about Zechariah and His wife in Luke 1: 5-7.

Facts	Zechariah	Elizabeth
Occupation (v. 15)		
Genealogy (descent) (v. 15)		
Children (v. 7)		
Spirituality "in eyes of the Lord"(v. 6)		
Age (v. 18)		
Contrast (with 430 years ago) (v. 6)		

A Holy Couple

In the Hebrew language of the Old Testament, "Zechariah" means, "Yahweh [the Lord] remembers."[5] This name certainly fits him as we will discover when we read about his vocation, his attitude and his marriage. (Please note, Zechariah is spelled differently depending on your Bible translation. The New Revised Standard Version, Catholic Edition (NRSVCE) and the New American Bible Revised Edition (NABRE, Lectionary version) use the name "Zechariah." In the original New both Testament Greek, the name was spelled "Zacharia" while "Zachary" was the name used in the old Douay-Rheims translation (based on St. Jerome's translation named after the cities where the translators lived in France). Other Bibles use the spelling "Zachariah." Please do not be distracted by any spelling differences. All Bibles are referring to the same person in Luke 1.)

"Elizabeth" is described as a "descendent of Aaron" (v. 5), which indicates she was a direct descendant of Aaron, the brother of Moses and Israel's first high priest (e.g., see Leviticus 8 and 9). This would indicate that Elizabeth and Zechariah came from a priestly family and John the Baptist would be born of full priestly descent.

The couple was described as "Righteous before God"(v. 6). Pope Benedict wrote "righteousness" means "the acceptance of God's will without reserve.[6] Thus, this dear couple was faithful to God and followed His commands in everything, even when life did not go as they had hoped.

The couple had prayed for something very precious to them. Luke 1:7 says it clearly, "They had no children." Zachariah and Elizabeth had remained faithful in serving God, even in the pain and suffering of childlessness. In Hebrew society childlessness was viewed as a disfavoring from God or even a punishment for sin (e.g., see Genesis 30: 2). Thus, Zechariah and Elizabeth likely felt lonely and even disgraced throughout their married life. Nevertheless, they chose to follow God with all their hearts in the midst of such circumstances. Other Bible couples, who were childless for many years, looked to God for help and received miracles, included, Abraham and Sarah (Genesis 11: 30; 15-17; 21:1-7), Isaac and Rebekah (Genesis 25: 21-24), Jacob and Rachel (Genesis 29-39; 35: 1-20), Manoah and the mother of Samson (Judges 13), and Elkanah and Hannah, the mother of Samuel (1 Samuel 1).

4. *CHOSEN BY LOT.* (a) Describe the two God-ordained events that happened to Zechariah in v. 8-9 and 10-11. (b) b) What was Zechariah's priestly order and what was their assignment (v. 5, 8, 9)?

_____
_____
_____
_____
_____
_____
_____

The Special Assignment

Zechariah belonged to the **priestly division of Abijah** (v. 5), and it was this division's turn to serve in the temple. At the time, there may have been up to 18,000 priests in Israel separated into 24 divisions of 1000 priests each.[7] Each division served in the temple twice per year for one week, and for the rest of the year they served in the synagogues in their own hometowns. The priests cast **lots** (v. 9) to determine their various duties, such as managing the temple, teaching the Scriptures or directing worship services.

A "lot" was similar to our dice—with colors instead of numbers and was cast in ancient practice to find guidance from God, when no prophet was available. Only one priest per day drew the lot for the special assignment of offering incense on the altar of incense in the temple, and he was allowed to do this holy task only once in his lifetime.[8] Many priests never had the opportunity. On this particular day, the lot fell to Zechariah— it would be a very special assignment - more than he could ever imagine.

Notes. **"At the time of the incense offering"** (v. 10) refers to the incense offered daily in the Holy Place of the temple as a symbol for prayers and worship ascending to God. The temple Holy Place was separated by a curtain or veil into two areas. Zechariah was offering incense in the front area, before the veil. In the back area, directly behind the veil, was the Holy of Holies, where a replica of the Ark of the Covenant containing Aaron's rod and the Ten Commandments were kept (the originals had been lost in the Babylon captivity).

"Standing on the right side of the altar" (v. 11) indicated a position of favor. Thus, the appearance of Gabriel on the right side would mean good news for Zechariah.[9] (Brown, 1993).

---

5. *THE ANGEL GABRIEL.* (a) Describe the angel who appeared to Zechariah (v. 12-13, 19-14). (b) Why would Zechariah be afraid? (c) How did Gabriel respond (v. 13)? (d) What similarities do you find with Gabriel's appearance to Daniel. See Daniel 8: 16-17 and Daniel 9: 20-23?

_____

_____

_____

_____

_____

_____

Daniel 8: 16-17. I heard a human voice by the Ulai, calling, "Gabriel, help this man [Daniel] understand the vision." 17 So he came near where I stood; and when he came, I became frightened and fell prostrate. (NRSVCE)

Daniel 9: 20-23. While I was speaking and was praying and confessing my sin and the sin of my people Israel and presenting my supplication before the Lord my God on behalf of the holy mountain of my God— 21 while I was speaking in prayer, the man Gabriel, whom I had seen before in a vision, came to me in swift flight at the time of the evening sacrifice. 22 He came and said to me, "Daniel, I have now come out to give you wisdom and understanding. 23 At the beginning of your supplications a word went out, and I have come to declare it, for you are greatly beloved. So consider the word and understand the vision... (NRSVCE)

6. GABRIEL'S MESSAGE. List the 8 prophecies Gabriel told Zechariah concerning the child that will be born to them (Luke 1: 14-21).

_____
_____
_____
_____
_____
_____
_____

The God-Incidence

It was a God-incidence, not a co-incidence! The chances were slim that Zechariah on any given day, in any given week, in any given year would draw the assignment to "enter the sanctuary of the Lord and offer incense," where he would pray for "the coming Messiah." But this day was different—it was in "the fullness of time" (Galatians 4:4) —God's time. It was the day the lot fell to Zechariah to serve in the Holy Place. It was the opportunity of a lifetime—the opportunity Zechariah had hoped for all of his life.!

As was customary, when a priest entered the Holy Place, the people waited outside the temple in prayer until the priest would come out and bless them. Now, Zechariah dressed in white robes of a priest, head covered and barefoot, entered the Holy Place. The golden candlestick was on one side and the table of showbread was on the other side. The altar of incense was before him. Moving his censor of incense back and forth, Zechariah began to pray. suddenly an angel appeared on the right side of the altar.

7. ZECHARIAH'S UNBELIEF. (a) How did Zechariah respond to Gabriel's promise of a son (v. 18)? (b) Why would Zechariah point out the impossibilities related to Elizabeth?

_____
_____
_____
_____
_____

Note. In New Testament Greek, "John" (v. 13) means "the Lord has shown favor" or "the Lord is gracious."[10] In the name John, God was showing great favor to Zechariah and Elizabeth. And to all of us.

Gabriel, The Might of God, Is No Small Cherub

There may have been many reasons why Zechariah did not believe Gabriel: (1) he may have lost hope in any change to his circumstances—after all, Elizabeth was old and past her time for having children, or (2) he may have been discouraged thinking that God didn't care about his personal life, or (3) he may have grown tired of praying—he had given up long ago and simply could not believe the possibility. Even the presence of a mighty angel didn't help.

Gabriel is no puny angel either. The name Gabriel in New Testament Greek means "the Might of God."[11] In an almost humorous way Gabriel used his *might* to teach Zechariah an important principle. Since Zechariah's name means, "the Lord remembers," **Zechariah would have a nine-month "silent retreat" to never to forget "the Lord remembers."**

Gabriel specifically appears in three other places in Scripture. In Daniel 8: 16-18 and in Daniel 9: 20-25, Gabriel gave Daniel insight about the coming of the Messiah. At that time, Daniel was in prayer at the evening sacrifice, became overwhelmed with fear, and found himself speechless in Gabriel's presence. Obviously, when Gabriel appears, he looks like his name implies—MIGHTY. He is sent from the presence of God and reflects God's magnificent glory. However, in Luke 1: 26-38, Gabriel announces the birth of the Messiah to sweet Blessed Mary and there the mighty Gabriel shows a gentle side.

8. *ZECHARIAH RETURNS HOME.* We know Zechariah returned home to tell Elizabeth about His shocking experience (v. 23-25), but the Scriptures do not give any details. (a) How to you think mute Zechariah greeted Elizabeth and told her about the message from Gabriel? (b) Can you envision how Elizabeth responded to Zechariah and to the Lord (v. 25)? (c) Why would Elizabeth stay secluded for 5 months before telling anyone about her miracle pregnancy?

_____

_____

_____

_____

_____

Joy Contained, the Proof Was in the Pudding (or Abdomen)

Although childless for most of their lives, Zechariah and Elizabeth remained faithful to the Lord, even when they gave up on God answering their prayers. For Zechariah and Elizabeth, childlessness had been shameful. In Jewish culture, children represented: (1) a legacy or sense of immortality, (2) social status or increase in wealth from having more workers to plant and harvest crops, and (3) social security or help for aging parents. We can only imagine the pity they endured from their neighbors.

Elizabeth may have waited to tell the neighbors about God's faithfulness because she wanted to keep the divine gift precious and secret [12]or she may have wanted to wait to show the visible proof of the miracle growing in her abdomen—a baby starts kicking near 16 to 20 weeks. Whatever the reason, we wonder, how could she contain her joy for five months? We don't know, but she did!

Pope John Paul II reminds us that children are a blessing and gift from the Lord, but we must remember not everyone has the opportunity to have children: ""It must not be forgotten, however, that, even when procreation is not possible, conjugal life does not for this reason lose its value." Those without children have "the occasion for other important services to the life of the human person—for example, adoption, various forms of educational work, assistance to other families and to poor or handicapped children."[13]

9. _PERSONAL REFLECTION._ This chapter takes us to meet Zechariah, Elizabeth and Gabriel plus offers historical background on the surprising message from God after 430 years of silence. Zechariah had given up on his prayers BUT God had a powerful message for him and for us. God hears. God answers. Don't give up on God. Jesus wants to share his joy with you. So, now is a good time to reflect on these first verses of our journey and write a new resolve to never give up on God. Pray with the following points:

(a) **Ask.** _Jesus, please give me a new and fresh prayer encounter with You. Fill me again with joy._

_____

_____

_____

(b) **Take Time.** Make a point to take some quiet time every day to listen to the Lord. Read these verses and other Scripture to stay connected to the joy of our Lord's first coming and His purposes. _Jesus, please speak to me through your Holy Word._

_____

_____

(c) **Converse.** Share with the Lord what you are waiting for. Then keep an open attitude to receive heavenly surprises and joy. _Jesus, I have given up on... Please give me new insight._

_____

_____

(d) **Praise.** Every day, in praise and worship, let the Lord know that you trust your life and circumstances to Him. _Lord Jesus, I praise you. You are King of Kings and Lord of Lords. I trust you..._

_____

_____

(e) **Journal.** Start an ADVENT PRAYER JOURNAL (any small notebook will do) to record your prayer with Jesus every day. Start journaling your response to what you learned in your journey with Jesus in Luke 1 from the perspective of Zechariah, Elizabeth, and Gabriel.

_____

_____

_____

The Lord Remembers

St. Jerome wrote about Zechariah: "Your prayer is heard...that is to say you are given more than you asked for. You prayed for the salvation of the people and you have been given the Precursor."[14]

Have you ever prayed for something so long that you gave up? Have you ever received more than you expected – just as you were about to give up? Zechariah had given up on having children. After all, he and Elizabeth were way past the age of the physical possibility, likely over 50 years of age. Yet, how appropriate was the meaning of Zechariah's name, "the Lord remembers," especially when Zechariah thinks the Lord forgot.

In Hebrew families at the time of Jesus, names were prayerfully chosen for children because Jewish parents believed that a God-given name would apply to the child's adult life. Somehow Zechariah forgot that his name was given to help him to recall, "the Lord remembers" him and his needs. We too must remember that nothing is impossible for God. He remembers us. He has plans that far exceed ours. He sees our every need.

Nineteenth century writer Alexander Whyte says we should keep praying even though answers are delayed because God has not forgotten us. Zechariah and Elizabeth teach us this principle:

"All these long past years of prayer, and waiting, and ceasing from prayer and turning to others, all that time Zacharias's answer had been ready before God, and had only been waiting till the best time for the answer to be sent down ... Other people's prayers and other people's providences may be so mixed up with yours that you will have to wait till their prayers, and their preparations and their providences are all as ripe and as ready as yours.

Zacharias and Elizabeth were ready long ago. But Joseph and Mary were not ready ... And thus, it was that, without knowing why, Zacharias and Elizabeth and John the Baptist had to wait in the hill country of Hebron till Joseph and Mary were made ready for the Divine predestination for their prayer, away north in Nazareth."[15]

10. YOUR PRAYER. Talk to Jesus about what actions you would like to take as a result of your time spent with Him this week and in this chapter. Focus your conversation on Luke 1: 1-25. Ask for more joy in His Word.
Then write your own prayer in the space below.

_____
_____
_____
_____
_____
_____
_____
_____
_____
_____

PRAYER EXAMPLE

Dear Jesus, thank you for the beautiful example of Zechariah and Elizabeth. They waited and You answered.

Thank you for the joy of Advent and your anticipated coming to earth.

Thank you for loving me and remembering me and the important things in my life, even when I think you have forgotten me. Nothing is too difficult for you.

Lord Jesus, draw me close to you. I give you all of my doubts, my disappointments and my lack of trust. Help me to pray always and never give up (Matthew 18: 1).

I want to listen to you more—in your Word—often and every day. Help me to take the time and to be quiet so I can hear you speak.

Jesus, I trust in You. I worship You.

2

Blessed Mary Meets Gabriel

Connection Question

We will read in the Scriptures that Jesus, Mary, and Joseph often traveled over 90 miles on foot. Have you ever tried to walk 90 miles?

The Annunciation[16]
by Domenico Beccafumi, 1545 AD
United States Public Domain

Chapter Two – Blessed Mary Meets Gabriel
The Annunciation of Jesus

Ninety Miles Down the Road

Put on your walking shoes. We're ready for quite a hike—at least 90 miles. Luke will take us from the Judean hill-country home of Zechariah and Elizabeth (about four miles outside of Jerusalem) down the road north to a small town in Galilee. This 90-mile walk will cover rocky terrain and hills, leading us into the district of Galilee to a village called Nazareth— the hometown of Mary and Joseph.

Chapter Two Questions

1. *LUKE 1: 26-38.* Please read Luke 1: 26-38. (a) Circle any reference to the time that has passed since Gabriel appeared to Zachariah – How much time has passed? (b) What is Mary's hometown? (c) What do you notice about Gabriel's appearance this time?

   _____

   _____

   _____

   _____

   _____

   _____

   _____

   _____

Luke 1: 26-38

In the sixth month, the angel Gabriel was sent by God to a town in Galilee called Nazareth, 27 to a virgin engaged to a man whose name was Joseph, of the house of David. The virgin's name was Mary. 28 And he came to her and said, "Greetings, favored one! The Lord is with you." 29 But she was much perplexed by his words and pondered what sort of greeting this might be. 30 The angel said to her, "Do not be afraid, Mary, for you have found favor with God. 31 And now, you will conceive in your womb and bear a son, and you will name him Jesus. 32 He will be great and will be called the Son of the Most High, and the Lord God will give to him the throne of his ancestor David. 33 He will reign over the house of Jacob forever, and of his kingdom there will be no end."

34 Mary said to the angel, "How can this be, since I am a virgin?"35 The angel said to her, "The Holy Spirit will come upon you, and the power of the Most High will overshadow you; therefore, the child to be born will be holy; he will be called Son of God. 36 And now, your relative Elizabeth in her old age has also conceived a son; and this is the sixth month for her who was said to be barren. 37 For nothing will be impossible with God." 38 Then Mary said, "Here am I, the servant of the Lord; let it be with me according to your word." Then the angel departed from her. NRSVCE

God is with His People, Even in the Most Unlikely Places

Nazareth, the hometown of Mary and Joseph was NOT the center of Jewish life or worship like Jerusalem was. It was NOT known for religion or learning. It was a small trading village located in a remote corner of Israel within the district of Galilee. The pace of life was slow. Nazareth was known to be a village where a nearby garrison of Roman soldiers and tradesmen frequented. In many ways, it was NOT a religious city, and this could explain why many Jews despised it. In John 1: 46, Nathanial said, "Can any good thing come out of Nazareth," likely referring to its unimportance, smallness, obscurity or even the immorality practiced by the nearby soldiers and pagan merchants. We will learn a great lesson in Nazareth: God can cause tremendous things and even miracles to happen in the most unlikely, remote, quiet or even ungodly places when people are open to Him and desiring to receive His graces. After all, this is the home of the Holy Family!

2. _THE VIRGIN._ List three quick facts you learn about Mary when she encountered Gabriel (v. 27)? (b) List one fact you learn about Joseph (v. 27).

_____

_____

_____

_____

_____

_____

_____

_____

_____

_____

Note. Mary means "Lady" in both Aramaic and in New Testament Greek.[17] It is a derivative of the Hebrew name Miriam, meaning "beloved of Yahweh" or "exalted one. Both fit the Blessed Mother.[18] Miriam in the Old Testament was the sister of Moses and Aaron. She led the women in praise and exaltation when God delivered Israel from the Egyptians at the parting of the Red Sea (see Exodus 15).

Engaged: The Betrothal

"Engaged" in v. 27 (NRSVCE) is more accurately translated "betrothed." The New Testament Greek word used here is pronounced _mnesthesomai_, and it means "to be remembered." In Jewish culture, a betrothal was a ceremony "to be remembered." Two people made a formal commitment to marry, somewhat like an engagement in American culture. However, when the betrothal was written and signed, it became a legally binding contract, like a marriage, but the couple would have no sexual intimacy until the actual marriage took place one year later.

The "betrothal" began with (1) a covenant in writing initiated by the groom's parents followed by (2) a meeting of the two families, plus (3) a gift of jewelry presented to the bride, (4) an announcement of intent by the groom, (5) sips from a cup of wine (first by the groom, then handed to the bride) signaling the bride's commitment to the covenant, and lastly (6) a ceremony with a priest where the groom offered payment or a dowry to the bride's family. The bride would live with her parents until the marriage ceremony.

During the year of betrothal, the couple would prepare their home and its furnishings. The betrothal could be broken only by divorce or death. The age of betrothal in the Hebrew culture was generally 14 -16 years of age for the woman and 18 - 24 years for the man. Thus, Mary was about 15 years old when Gabriel appeared to her.[19]

3. GABRIEL. (a) How did Gabriel greet Mary (v. 28-30)? (b) How did Mary respond (v. 30).

_____

_____

_____

_____

_____

_____

_____

_____

_____

_____

Note. "Of the House of David" points to the Old Testament prophecies concerning the coming of the Messiah. In 2 Samuel 7:12-13, God said to David, "When your days are complete and you lie down with your ancestors, I will raise up your offspring after you, who will come forth from your body, and I will establish his kingdom…and I will establish the throne of his kingdom forever." The establishment of David's throne, called the "Davidic Covenant," promised that the Messiah would come from the lineage of David and He would reign forever. The Jewish people understood this important Old Testament prophecy and they were looking for the Messiah to come and reign forever. St. Joseph was a descendent of David (Matthew 1: 6-16). Wow! God was about to fulfill the Old Testament prophecies. (See Psalm 89: 3-4, Psalm 132: 11, Isaiah 9: 6-7, and Isaiah 11:1-2 for additional prophecies of the Messiah coming from the lineage of David and reigning forever.)

Hail Mary – Joy Be with You

In v. 28, "Greetings" (or "Hail" in some translations) literally means, "rejoice" or "joy be with you." Thus, Gabriel's message was meant to give Mary great joy. Gabriel affirmed the incarnation with "The Lord is with you" (v. 28). The divine was about to take on humanity: "The *Holy Spirit will come upon you*"(v. 35), *eperchomai* in New Testament Greek, means God will invade you and that is just what happened. The Holy Spirit came upon Mary, invaded her body, and filled her presence with the Savior Jesus Christ. St. Augustine said of Mary at the incarnation, "the Holy Spirit … is more with you than he is with me: he is in your heart, he takes shape within you, he fills your soul, he is in your womb. "[20]

Mary was favored and chosen by God, but this did not exempt her from pain and suffering. Actually, the immediate result of the heavenly visitation of Gabriel likely brought on ridicule from neighbors and even temporary rejection by Joseph (e.g., Matthew 1: 19). But, Mary's faithfulness and submission to God brought the greatest gift ever to mankind---the birth of Jesus Christ, our Savior. Mary participated in God's plan with trust even when it meant suffering. THE LORD WAS WITH HER!

Remember, THE LORD IS WITH YOU today through the power of the Holy Spirit. You can choose to trust the Lord and His Words, as Mary did. You can choose to give Him your fears and troubles, as Mary did. You can be open to receive His message to YOU, as Mary did. You can be filled with His JOY if you ask the Holy Spirit to fill you.

4. GABRIEL'S MESSAGE. (a) Using the chart below, list the three instructions Gabriel gave Mary and (b) list the five prophecies he spoke concerning her son Jesus? Use the following chart to record your answers.

Three Instructions to Mary (v. 31)	Five prophecies about Jesus (v. 32-33)
1.	1.
2.	2.
3.	3.
	4.
	5.

Jesus, Named After His Heavenly Father

Do you have a family member named after your father or your mother?   God does!   God the Father gave the Son his name! **The Name *Jesus*** is translated from the Hebrew name *Yeshua,* which is a derivative of *Yahweh.* *Yahweh* was the Most Holy Name of God in the Old Testament—too holy for the Hebrews to pronounce aloud. Thus the message would be clear: *Yahweh God* would name His son *Yeshua* after himself. **Truly, Jesus would be the Son of God**.

In New Testament Greek (the original language of much of the New Testament), the **name *Jesus*** is actually *Joshua* and it means *"**God saves**"* (*Catechism of the Catholic Church* [CCC], 430). The Jewish people knew the name *Joshua* from their history because *Joshua* was the one who helped Moses lead the people out of slavery and into the Promised Land (Joshua 1: 1-18).   They knew the name "Jesus" pointed to the One who would bring salvation. *The Catechism of the Catholic Church* explains:

> The **name Jesus** "expresses both his identity and his mission. Since God alone can forgive sins, it is God who, in Jesus his eternal Son made man, will save his people from their sins" … "It is this divine name that alone brings salvation, and henceforth all can invoke his name, for Jesus united himself to all men through his Incarnation, so that 'there is no other name under heaven given among men by which we must be saved.'"[21]

5. VIRGIN BIRTH. (a) What Old Testament prophecy from Isaiah 7:14 was about to be fulfilled in Luke 1: 34-55? (b) Why does the virgin birth play an essential role in all Christian faith and doctrine? (c) Since God said it would happen and it did, why do some people find it hard to believe Jesus Christ was born of a Virgin?

_____

_____

_____

_____

_____

_____

_____

Isaiah 7: 14. Therefore the Lord Himself will give you a sign: Behold, a virgin will be with child and bear a son, and she will call His named Immanuel (God with us).

God Became Man – The Incarnation

Why do people find it so hard to believe in the virgin birth? The virgin birth and incarnation are essential parts of our Christian faith. The *incarnation* means God became man, reaching out to mankind. In no other religion does God "become flesh" (John 1: 14), "accept the limitations of humanity," come to earth to show His love, and then die for the sins of all.[22] God Himself is the Father of Jesus and that is why the virgin birth, prophesied through Isaiah nearly 740 years earlier, is an essential part of the Christian faith.

St. Augustine says even when we cannot understand this miracle, "Let us grant that God can do something which we confess we cannot fathom. In such matters, the whole explanation of the deed is in the power of the Doer."[23] *The Catechism of the Catholic Church* stresses the importance of the incarnation: "From the first formulations of faith, the Church has confessed that Jesus was conceived solely by the power of the Holy Spirit in the womb of the Virgin Mary, affirming also the corporeal aspect of this event: Jesus was conceived by the Holy Spirit without human seed."[24] God showed His great love for us...for YOU!

6. MARY'S QUESTION, GABRIEL'S ANSWER. (a) What was Mary's question to Gabriel (v. 34-35) and how did Gabriel respond(v. 37)? (b) How is Mary's question: "How can this be since I am a virgin?" (v. 34-45,) different from Zechariah's question (v. 18), "How will I know"? (c) Why do you think Gabriel responded differently to Mary than he did to Zechariah?

_____

_____

_____

_____

_____

_____

_____

Note. **May it be done to me according to your word** was Mary's "yes"—it was her statement of consent and cooperation with the *Word of God* to become the mother of Jesus. "Rightly, therefore, the [Church] Fathers see Mary not merely as passively engaged by God, but as freely cooperating in the work of man's salvation through faith and obedience."[25] Mary's heart readily received the Word from God because she was already in deep communion with God and her will was to do his will. Deep communion is the place of rest and surrender of control and it's where we all need to aim to live.

7. _MARY ACTS._ Describe how these four words depict Mary's prayerful attitude and actions before her "yes" of Luke 1: 28-32: "listen," "ponder," "dialogue," and "surrender?

Elizabeth's Insights in Mary's Greeting	
v. 28 LISTEN	
v.29 PONDER	
v.34 DIALOGUE	
v. 38 SURRENDER	

Zechariah Asked for a Sign, Mary Asked for Understanding

Was there a difference between Zechariah's and Mary's question to Gabriel? Gabriel certainly responded differently to 'Mary than he did to Zechariah. There are two key phrases that show the difference between Zechariah's question of unbelief and Mary's question for understanding. Zechariah asked, "HOW WILL I KNOW THIS IS SO?" He asked for a sign and next pointed out the obstacles ("_I am an old man; my wife is getting on in years_"). On the other hand, Mary asked for understanding, "HOW CAN THIS BE?" She was defending her betrothal virginity and asked a legitimate question to try to grasp how an event such as this could happen. Zechariah got his sign— a silent retreat for NINE months: "But now, because you did not believe my words, which will be fulfilled in their time, you will become mute, unable to speak, until the day these things occur" (Luke 1: 20). Mary got her answer— "The Holy Spirit will come upon you" (Luke 1: 35) and HE DID!

Mary's response gives us an example of how to respond in times of stress, anxiety or trouble. We can seek the will of God and dialogue with Him about any problem. Mary did not ask for a sign. She simply asked a question because she was committed to remaining a virgin in her betrothal. Mary was not thoughtless, but rather listened carefully and pondered what she could not understand. To ponder means _to consider with deep dialogue._

After the dialogue, Mary responded with what is called, "**_Mary's Fiat._**" The word "fiat" in Latin is the first word of verse 38 in St. Jerome's Latin translation of the Bible and it means "let it be." This was Mary's "YES." After listening, pondering and engaging in dialogue, she surrendered to God's will for her life saying, "Let it be done to me according to your word."

Mary included these words at the end of her fiat: "Here am I, the servant [handmaid] of the Lord." "Servant" ("*doulet*" in New Testament Greek) refers to one who is in chosen surrender. So, Mary received the Word of God and humbly surrendered and entrusted herself to God's will for her life.

Mary gives us this example of how to seek and accept God's will in these four words:

- **Listen** — Be fully present to God and allow the Word of God to speak to your mind and heart,

- **Ponder** — Meditate on and mull over the Word of God,

- **Dialogue** — Talk to God to gain understanding and wait for His answer in prayerful expectation, not scoffing at God or your circumstances, and

- **Surrender** — Tell God you trust your life to Him with humility and faithfulness, not in mindlessness but with full trust in His ultimate plan and praise Him for His greatness.

Mary's life also shows us that God calls unlikely candidates to do His will. Mary was poor, young and a woman. Her "*YES*" teaches us to say, "yes," even when we feel completely unworthy, unprepared, unskilled or unlikely to be the best one to do the job. Our service starts when we respond with Mary, **"Yes, Lord, I place my trust in you. Yes, Lord,** *let it be done with me according to Your Word.* **Yes, Lord, I am your servant."**

8. TIMING OF THE ANNUNCIATION. When do you think, "the Holy Spirit came upon Mary," (v. 35) to overshadow her with our Savior?

_____

_____

_____

_____

_____

_____

God Became Man When the Angel Departed

Some may wonder when this marvelous act of God happened. Archbishop Alban Goodier, S.J. suggests the timing of when the Holy Spirit came upon Mary:

"The Angel departed with his message of joy, but God did not depart. That instant He began His life as man on earth, the entire possession of her whom He had chosen for His very own. Mary at that moment, the little child lost in bewildering adoration, is the joy of mankind, the joy of all the world, the joy of all the angels, the joy of God the Father, the joy of God the Son, the joy of God the Holy Spirit; and she is the joy of each individual soul that comes into the world and realizes even a little what it possesses in her." [26]

Mary abandoned herself to God and God gave her more than she had ever imagined. St. Josemaria Escriva (1973) shares what God spoke to him during a rough time in his life and gives us a prayer of abandonment based on Mary's *YES:*

"Father, I am having a very rough time. In answer, God whispered into my ear, 'take upon your shoulders a small part of the cross, just a tiny part. And if you can't manage that then leave it entirely on the strong shoulders of My Son Jesus. Then don't worry about anything anymore. From this moment on, repeat: 'My Lord and My God, into your hands I abandon the past, and the present, and the future, what is small and what is great, what amounts to a lot, things temporal and things eternal.'"[27]

9. _MEDITATION._ Please prayerfully meditate on the marvelous encounter between the Angel Gabriel and Mary in "the Annunciation." Picture yourself in the scene with Mary. How would she feel when she hears she will be the mother of the long-awaited Savior? How will she contain the joy? Then allow yourself to be guided by these prompts:

(a) **Imagine yourself** as a humble one, like Mary — living in the obscurity of Nazareth. Yet, you are open to all the ways of God. God shares His joy with you.

_____

_____

_____

(b) **Listen to the message** spoken to you. YOUR SAVIOR IS COME. Your joy overflows.

_____

_____

_____

(c) **Open your heart,** Jesus wants to come ever more deeply into your life. Hear the Good News He is announcing to you. God became man to show his Love for you. Jesus died for your sins. God is with you! He loves you. Receive His joy.

_____

_____

_____

(d) **Trust the Lord!** Join Mary in her YES to God, "Let it be with me according to your Word." I surrender my life to you. I trust you Father, Son and Holy Spirit. I give you the controls of my life.

_____

_____

_____

10. *PERSONAL PRAYER RESPONSE.* Consider what God has spoken to you from this beautiful section of Scripture on the *Annunciation*. Ask Him to help you share in the joy of the incarnation and Mary's fiat. Then write a simple prayer of joyful response.

_____

_____

_____

_____

_____

_____

_____

_____

_____

_____

_____

_____

PRAYER EXAMPLE

Dear Lord Jesus,

Thank you for the Blessed Virgin Mary and her joyful "fiat" — *YES*. I too desire to surrender my life to YOU—to your plans for me, to your will.

I hear your call and I want to follow. Please help me to be present to you daily and to **listen** for your voice in your Word. When I fail to listen, forgive me. When I fail to follow, lead me back. When I fail to receive your joy, remind me that you are always there.

Oh Lord, help me to take time to **ponder** and meditate on these beautiful verses about your coming. What I do not understand, I promise to **dialogue** with you. I **surrender** my problems to you. "Nothing is impossible for YOU."

Yes, I place my trust in You -- Jesus, the Baby in the manger, my God and my King. I give you my life anew today. I receive your joy.

I will serve you and obey you. I wait patiently for your plans to unfold in my life. Jesus, Christ, you are my Savior and Lord. I love YOU. Jesus, I trust in YOU…

3

Mary Visits Elizabeth – The Visitation

Connection Question

Why is it helpful to share your emotions – joys or anxieties, inspirations or uncertainties, successes or failures – with another who understands you? Who do you go to for sharing life's uncertainties?

The Visitation[28]
by Philippe de Champaigne, 1602-1674
United States Public Domain

Chapter Three - Mary Visits Elizabeth
The Visitation

Back to the Hill Country of Judea

Luke takes us from Nazareth back down the 90-mile road to the Hill Country of Judea, near Jerusalem. We will drop in on the very special visit that Mary makes to her cousin Elizabeth. Both women are with child, both are rejoicing over the births to come, and both are thrilled to see each other. God knew Mary and Elizabeth would need to share their joys, their uncertainties, their pregnancies and their very lives with each other at this time. As you might remember, Gabriel told Mary, "And now, your relative Elizabeth in her old age has also conceived a son; and this is the sixth month for her who was said to be barren. For nothing will be impossible with God (v. 36)." Isn't it wonderful to consider that God knows our needs in advance, especially our needs for deep sharing and spiritual fellowship?

Chapter Three Questions

1. *LUKE 1: 36-56.* Please read Luke 1 36-56 aloud and underline any words or phrases that indicate Mary and Elizabeth's emotions at this meeting. Share what you noted.

_____

_____

_____

_____

_____

_____

_____

Luke 1: 36-56

And now, your relative Elizabeth in her old age has also conceived a son; and this is the sixth month for her who was said to be barren. [37]For nothing will be impossible with God." [38] Then Mary said, "Here am I, the servant of the Lord; let it be with me according to your word." Then the angel departed from her. [39] In those days Mary set out and went with haste to a Judean town in the hill country, [40] where she entered the house of Zechariah and greeted Elizabeth. [41]When Elizabeth heard Mary's greeting, the child leaped in her womb. And Elizabeth was filled with the Holy Spirit [42] and exclaimed with a loud cry, "Blessed are you among women, and blessed is the fruit of your womb. [43]And why has this happened to me, that the mother of my Lord comes to me? [44] For as soon as I heard the sound of your greeting, the child in my womb leaped for joy. [45]And blessed is she who believed that there would be a fulfillment of what was spoken to her by the Lord." [46]And Mary said,

"My soul magnifies the Lord, [47]and my spirit rejoices in God my Savior, [48]for he has looked with favor on the lowliness of his servant. Surely, from now on all generations will call me blessed; [49]for the Mighty One has done great things for me, and holy is his name. [50]His mercy is for those who fear him from generation to generation. [51] He has shown strength with his arm; he has scattered the proud in the thoughts of their hearts. [52] He has brought down the powerful from their thrones and lifted up the lowly; [53]he has filled the hungry with good things and sent the rich away empty. [54] He has helped his servant Israel, in remembrance of his mercy, [55]according to the promise he made to our ancestors, to Abraham and to his descendants forever."

[56]And Mary remained with her about three months and then returned to her home

2. _GABRIEL'S NEWS ABOUT ELIZABETH._ (a) According to v. 36-39, what did Gabriel tell Mary about Elizabeth and why would this be such special news for Mary? (b) Why do you think Mary was in such a hurry (e.g., "left in haste," v. 39)?

_____

_____

_____

_____

_____

_____

_____

Mary Went with Haste to See Elizabeth

Mary had a long distance to travel in order to visit Elizabeth. The distance from Nazareth to the hill country of Judah, as mentioned earlier, was about 90 miles — up to a four-day journey for a pregnant young woman. At that time, people either traveled on foot or joined caravans of fellow travelers when making long journeys. We would expect that Mary joined such a caravan when she left Nazareth. Can't you just feel Mary's joy and wonder and need to fellowship with her cousin Elizabeth about the wonderful news they both would share regarding the next events on God's calendar?

3. _THE GREETING._ (a) According to v. 41, what happened to Elizabeth when she heard Mary's greeting? (b) How did Elizabeth respond to Mary (v. 42)?

_____

_____

_____

_____

_____

_____

_____

_____

_____

Note. "The infant leaped in her womb" (v. 41) is described by St Ambrose as John the Baptist's awareness of grace: "Elizabeth is the first to hear Mary's voice, but John is the first to be aware of grace. She hears with the ears of the body, but he leaps for joy at the meaning of the mystery. She is aware of Mary's presence, but he is aware of the Lord…a woman aware of a woman's presence, the forerunner aware of the pledge of our salvation"[29] Both were filled with the Holy Spirit!

---

4. _HOLY SPIRIT REALIZATIONS._ (a) Do you think Elizabeth was expecting Mary to visit her? (b) Please list the insights Elizabeth had in Mary's greeting.

Elizabeth's Insights in Mary's Greeting	
v. 42	
v. 43	
v. 44	
v. 45	

<u>5.</u> <u>***THE BLESSED VISIT.***</u> (a) Do you think Elizabeth was expecting Mary (v. 43)? Why or Why not? (b) Why do you think Elizabeth praised Mary for believing "there would be a fulfillment of what was spoken to her by the Lord?" (Hint: Remember what happened to Zechariah when he did NOT believe.) (c) How did Elizabeth know that Mary was the mother of "my Lord"?

_____

_____

_____

_____

_____

_____

_____

_____

<u>6. *THE MAGNIFICAT.*</u>   Please read Luke 1: 46-55 again—the section called the Magnificat. Circle any words or phrases that catch your attention. Share your thoughts.

_____

_____

_____

_____

_____

_____

_____

_____

_____

The Magnificat— Mary's Song of Praise

Jesus was identified as "the Lord," even before His birth. Gabriel had promised it. He told Zechariah that John would "prepare a people fit for the Lord" (Luke 1: 17). The Holy Spirit obviously had revealed it to Elizabeth, possibly at the moment she heard Mary's greeting and was filled with the Holy Spirit (v. 41). She also praised Mary's faith. Zachariah would have communicated to her (possibly by writing on a tablet) that he was struck mute because he did not believe the heavenly message delivered by Gabriel.

Mary's beautiful words of praise in Luke 1: 46-56 make up what is called **The Magnificat** or **The Song of Mary.** This song gets its name from St. Jerome's Latin translation of the Bible where the first word in Latin in v. 46 is *Magnificat,* which is translated **"my soul magnifies."** The New Revised Standard Version Catholic Edition (NRSVCE) actually uses the word "magnifies" instead of "proclaims" or "glorifies" as other translations use. *The Magnificat* in Luke 1: 46-56 is also called a *canticle* **("canticulum" in Latin),** which by definition is a **liturgical song, especially from a Biblical text.**[30] The *Magnificat* is sung by the Catholic Church every evening at *Vespers* in the *Liturgy of the Hours* and it reflects themes from many Old Testament Scriptures, especially from Hannah's prayer in 1 Samuel 2.

7. MAGNIFICAT THEMES. To further reflect on the meaning of the Magnificat canticle, please underline the phrases from Hannah's prayer in 1 Samuel 2: 1-10 that seem to match the major themes in Mary's canticle. Share your thoughts.

_____
_____
_____
_____
_____
_____
_____
_____
_____

1 Samuel 2: 1-10. Hannah prayed and said, [1]"My heart exults in the Lord; my strength is exalted in my God. My mouth derides my enemies, because I rejoice in my victory. [2] "There is no Holy One like the Lord, no one besides you; there is no Rock like our God. [3] Talk no more so very proudly, let not arrogance come from your mouth; for the Lord is a God of knowledge, and by him actions are weighed. [4] The bows of the mighty are broken, but the feeble gird on strength. [5]

Those who were full have hired themselves out for bread, but those who were hungry are fat with spoil. The barren has borne seven, but she who has many children is forlorn. ⁶ The Lord kills and brings to life; he brings down to Sheol and raises up. ⁷ The Lord makes poor and makes rich; he brings low, he also exalts. ⁸ He raises up the poor from the dust; he lifts the needy from the ash heap, to make them sit with princes and inherit a seat of honor. For the pillars of the earth are the Lord's, and on them he has set the world. ⁹ "He will guard the feet of his faithful ones, but the wicked shall be cut off in darkness; for not by might does one prevail. ¹⁰ The Lord! His adversaries shall be shattered; the *Most High* will thunder in heaven. The Lord will judge the ends of the earth; he will give strength to his king and exalt the power of his anointed."

8. MAGNIFICAT AND SCRIPTURE. (a) Read each of the following Scriptures and circle any words that are similar to words found in Mary's *Magnificat.* (b) What do you learn about Mary when you consider her *Magnificat* response includes words and phrases from several Psalms and other Old Testament Scriptures?

_____
_____
_____
_____
_____
_____
_____
_____

Words from Old Testament Scriptures in Mary's Magnificat

- **Psalm 34: 2.** My soul makes its boast in the Lord; let the humble hear and be glad. (Luke 1:46)

- **Psalm 35: 9.** Then my soul shall rejoice in the Lord, exulting in his deliverance. (Luke 1:47)

- **Psalm 138: 6.** For though the Lord is high, he regards the lowly; but the haughty he perceives from far away. (Luke 1:48)

- **Psalm 103: 17.** But the steadfast love of the Lord is from everlasting to everlasting on those who fear him, and his righteousness to children's children. (Luke 1:50)

- **Psalm 107:9.** For he satisfies the thirsty, and the hungry he fills with good things. (Luke 1: 53)

- **Psalm 132: 11.** The Lord swore to David a sure oath from which he will not turn back: "One of the sons of your body I will set on your throne. (Luke 1: 54-55)

- **Job 5: 11.** He sets on high those who are lowly, and those who mourn are lifted to safety.... (Luke 1: 52)

Mary Loved Scripture

It is obvious from the language Mary used in the *Magnificat* that she was trained in the Old Testament Scriptures, most likely by her parents (Anne and Joachim) and by temple teachers. She knew the Scriptures by heart so, when her heart was leaping with joy, she naturally used the same words to praise God. The WORD of God was never far from Mary's lips. The Most Rev. Alban Goodier, S. J. explains: "Here [in Scripture] more than anywhere else we are able to detect the soul of Our Lady; here we have her authentic biography in the language with which her lips are the most familiar."[31]

In Mary's Magnificat, we get to read her song of joy and praise to God for his powerful arm in choosing her—a lowly handmaid— and raising her up to be called "blessed" by all generations. She sings of God's mercy toward her and toward all who do not deserve His kindness and grace. She exalts in God's powerful might that both enthrones and dethrones kings. She praises His justice toward those who are prideful in riches. She rejoices in God's faithfulness for keeping His promises to Abraham and the fathers of our faith. She points out three transformations that will come through Jesus Christ as He reigns in His kingdom: **(1) A moral transformation**—Jesus scatters the proud-hearted, so they see themselves for who they are, **(2) A social transformation**—Jesus exalts the humble and casts down the godless and mighty from their thrones, and **(3) An economic transformation**—Jesus fills the hungry—physically and spiritually, but sends the satiated rich, filled on worldly pursuits, away empty.[32]

Mary's upbringing as a devout and religious Hebrew taught her to care for the poor and afflicted, which can be observed in Luke 1: 48, 52, and 53. Mary's prophetic words, "He has thrown down rulers...lifted up the lowly, the hungry He has filled with good things and the rich He has sent away empty" were fulfilled in a very literal way, as John Brook points out:

It was the wealthy and religious elite of Israel who rejected Jesus and, in the end, were sent away empty. They refused the salvation offered by God and they ended up with nothing. It was the starving, the poor, who welcomed Jesus, believed in him, and were filled with the good things God gave in Christ, the gifts of forgiveness and the Holy Spirit. In the life of the kingdom, it is those who continue to 'hunger and thirst after righteousness' who will be filled. It is those who are poor in spirit, those who know their need of God, who will be satisfied.[33]

9. _MARY'S TONE._ (a) What would you say is the tone of Mary's song (v. 47)? (b) How did Elizabeth further bring out Mary's joy? (c) How do others bring out your joy?

_____

_____

_____

_____

_____

_____

_____

A Joy-filled Song of Humility, Gratitude and Adoration

Mary skipped for joy as she proclaimed the goodness of God. In Luke 1: 47 she says, "my spirit **rejoices** in God, my Savior." The New Testament Greek word translated "rejoice" is pronounced _"agalliao,"_ and it means to jump for joy, to be exceedingly glad, or to show ecstatic joy by leaping and skipping."[34] So, we can say, "**The Magnificat"** _is_ **a joy-filled song of praise.** It expresses Mary's thanksgiving, humility and worship for the great things God has done. Also, she is thrilled to be with Elizabeth who shares her joy and together, they are exceedingly glad.

The _Catechism of the Catholic Church_ explains that Mary's Magnificat adores God:

To adore God is to acknowledge, in respect and absolute submission, the "nothingness of the creature" who would not exist but for God. To adore God is to praise and exalt him and to humble oneself, as Mary did in the Magnificat, confessing with gratitude that he has done great things and holy is his name. The worship of the one God sets man free from turning in on himself, from the slavery of sin and the idolatry of the world.[35]

Let us worship the Father and Jesus Christ, the Son, our Lord and Savior.

10. FELLOWSHIP. (a) How long did Mary stay with Elizabeth (v. 56)? (b)What value would Elizabeth's love, support and confirmation have for Mary? (c) What do you suppose Mary and Elizabeth talked about for three months? (d) List what Mary and Elizabeth had in common in spite of their age differences.

_____

_____

_____

_____

_____

_____

Mary Returned Home

We do not know if Mary stayed for the birth of John the Baptist. By omitting any reference to Mary at the birth of John, Luke seems to indicate that she left quickly near the time of the birth. She knew there would be a convergence of the Jewish neighborhood and family at Zechariah's house for John's arrival. Plus, Mary would have been eager to return home as soon as her abdomen pushed outward. She would want to share everything with Joseph and her parents.

 For the three-month visit, we can only imagine the comfort Mary and Elizabeth must have been to each other. They likely talked of the Scriptures to be fulfilled because they knew well the promises regarding the Messiah and the one who would precede Him. They probably shared the stories about Gabriel as each had been changed by his message and they would have known of his former visitations recorded in Daniel 9: 20-21.

Elizabeth would have heard only about Gabriel through Zechariah, so she would have leaned on every word Mary shared. Elizabeth was old, so Mary probably helped her with the discomforts of pregnancy, the cooking and even the errands; yet, Elizabeth would have shared so much about life with Mary. They probably made baby clothes and talked of womanly things. What wonderful conversation Mary and Elizabeth must have shared, what fun they must have experienced, and what joy they must have felt. After all, the man in the house was speechless! Gabriel had given him a nine-month silent retreat.

11. MEDITATION. Let's take time to reflect on the wonderful, holy visit of Mary to Elizabeth. Can you sense the joy, excitement and bewilderment they shared? Prayerfully consider these applications and responses for your life:

(a) **New Joy.** Is your heart open to receive new joy from Jesus every day? In prayer, ask Him for more joy.

_____

_____

(b) **Rejoicing in Jesus.** Are you rejoicing in the Lord? Are you praising Him with joy? Since gratitude often precedes genuine joyfulness, make it your goal to thank the Lord every day for all he has done for you? Fr. Francis Fernandez tells us to rejoice every day because Jesus is very near to us and wants to be even nearer during the season of Advent: *This is also the joy of Advent, and that of every day. Jesus is very near us. He is nearer every day. Joy is to possess Jesus; unhappiness is to lose Him…To find Christ and to remain in his company, is to possess a deep happiness which is new every day.*[36]

_____

_____

(c) **Quiet Prayer Time.** Are you spending a quiet time in prayer with Jesus every day?

_____

(d) **Sharing Joys.** Are you sharing your joys and encouraging other women just as Mary and Elizabeth did for each other?

_____

_____

(e) **Encourage Others.** Who would be the Elizabeth's or Mary's in your life? Who has God invited you to mentor or encourage? Who will you reach out to this week that might need your encouragement?

_____

_____

12. _MY PERSONAL PRAYER RESPONSE_. Talk to the Lord about your response to the joyful Visitation message. Then write a prayer from you heart based on the verses from this section of Scripture. See the following example.

_____

_____

_____

_____

_____

_____

_____

_____

PRAYER EXAMPLE

Dear Lord Jesus,

Thank you for the Visitation and the joy Mary and Elizabeth shared. Thank you for creating us to need Holy Spirit-filled relationships and fellowship with others.

Thank you for calling me to share my life with others. I ask you to bring those into my life to be my friend and mentor or to whom I can mentor, especially to share the joy of my faith and knowing you as my Savior.

Thank you for the joy-filled Magnificat praises of Mary. Help me to praise you with the Magnificat often. Thank you for all the goodness you have shown family and myself.

Thank you, Jesus. You are faithful to all your promises and you are merciful. Even when I don't feel like it, I can be confident you are with me always and You hear my prayers. I receive Your joy and hope.

Lord Jesus, I give my life to you today and receive you as Lord and Savior. May I serve You all the days of my life. Now, I offer this prayer for … (include your petitions). Close with the _Magnificat_ Prayer.

The Magnificat

My soul proclaims [magnifies] the greatness of the Lord,

My spirit rejoices in God my savior for he has looked with favor on his lowly servant.

From this day, all generations will call me blessed:
The Almighty has done great things for me, and holy is His name.

He has mercy on those who fear him in every generation.

He has shown the strength of his arm, He has scattered the proud in their conceit.

He has cast down the mighty from their thrones and has lifted up the lowly.

He has filled the hungry with good things, and the rich he has sent away empty.

He has come to the help of his servant Israel for he remembered his promise of mercy, the promise he made to our fathers, to Abraham and to his children forever.

Glory to the Father, and to the Son,
and to the Holy Spirit,
as it was in the beginning,
is now,
and will be forever.
Amen.

4

John the Baptist is Born – Zechariah's Tongue is Loosed

Connection Question

Do you know what your name means?

The Birth of John the Baptist[37]
Zechariah wrote, "His name is John."
by Jacopo Pontormo, 1526, United States Public Domain

Chapter Four - John the Baptist Born
Zechariah's Tongue Loosed

The Birth and Circumcision of John the Baptist

The birth of the Savior is imminent, but first comes the precursor, "the one who would go before Him in the spirit and power of Elijah" (Luke 1:17). That is where Luke takes us next and what an exciting event for us to drop in on! Can't you just picture yourself as one of the neighbors who has come to help name the baby born to the old priest Zechariah and his aged wife Elizabeth. Can you hear yourself say, "This must be some kind of child—a miracle baby! What a blessing from the Lord for Elizabeth! Poor old Zechariah was struck mute the last time he went up to serve in the temple."

So, let's head to the celebration.

Chapter One Questions

1. JOHN'S BIRTH. (a) Read Luke 1: 55-66 and circle any phrases that describe the important events taking place. (b) Why did fear come upon all the neighbors?

_____
_____
_____
_____
_____
_____
_____
_____
_____

Luke 1: 56-66

56 And Mary remained with her about three months and then returned to her home. 57 Now the time came for Elizabeth to give birth, and she bore a son. 58 Her neighbors and relatives heard that the Lord had shown his great mercy to her, and they rejoiced with her. 59 On the eighth day they came to circumcise the child, and they were going to name him Zechariah after his father. 60 But his mother said, "No; he is to be called John." 61 They said to her, "None of your relatives has this name." 62 Then they began motioning to his father to find out what name he wanted to give him. 63 He asked for a writing tablet and wrote, "His name is John." And all of them were amazed. 64 Immediately his mouth was opened and his tongue freed, and he began to speak, praising God. 65 Fear came over all their neighbors, and all these things were talked about throughout the entire hill country of Judea. 66 All who heard them pondered them and said, "What then will this child become?" For, indeed, the hand of the Lord was with him. NRSVCE

2. _MARY RETURNED HOME._ (a)According to v. 56, how long did Mary stay with Elizabeth? (b) Why do you think she left when she did?

_____
_____
_____
_____
_____
_____
_____

The Three-Month Visit

According to Scripture, Mary remained with Elizabeth about three months and then returned to her home. We don't know if Mary stayed for the birth of Elizabeth and Zechariah's baby. Many ancient paintings show Mary holding John the Baptist. We don't know why Mary left after only three months. Luke doesn't tell us! We do know that after Mary left Elizabeth and returned home, she was "found with child," likely meaning neighbors, family and friends found out Mary was pregnant (Matthew 1:18).

3. _THE NEIGHBORS._ How did the neighbors and relatives respond when they heard of John's birth (v. 58)?

_____

_____

_____

_____

_____

_____

> **Note. John means "God is gracious"** and that was the name God chose, as spoken to Zechariah by the Angel **Gabriel.** Obviously, the name was well chosen. John would be a "great source of grace." He would be the forerunner of Christ, "preparing the way" before Him (Malachi 3: 1, Luke 1: 76) and announcing God's grace "to those who sit in darkness" (Luke 1: 79) "to give His people knowledge of salvation through the forgiveness of their sins" (Luke 1:77). John's message is and was: "Repent of your sins and believe the Good News. The Lord has come to save you" (Luke 3: 3 and17-18). That's the grace of God, and we don't deserve it.

4. _THE CONVENANT CEREMONY._ (a) In what way did the naming of the newborn take place (v. 59)? (b) How were Gabriel's words to Zechariah in Luke 1: 14, "Many will rejoice to see His birth" fulfilled? (c) Read Genesis 17: 7-14 and explain the meaning of circumcision to the Hebrew people. (d) What similarities and differences do you notice between the Sacrament of Baptism and the Jewish Circumcision of John?

_____

_____

_____

_____

_____

_____

Genesis 17: 7, 10-14. God said to Abraham: "I will maintain my covenant with you and your descendants after you throughout the ages as an everlasting pact to be your God and the God of your descendants after you... 10 This is my covenant, which you shall keep, between me and you and your offspring after you: Every male among you shall be circumcised. 11You shall circumcise the flesh of your foreskins, and it shall be a sign of the covenant between me and you. 12Throughout your generations every male among you shall be circumcised when he is eight days old, including the slave born in your house and the one bought with your money from any foreigner who is not of your offspring. [13]Both the slave born in your house and the one bought with your money must be circumcised. So shall my covenant be in your flesh an everlasting covenant. [14]Any uncircumcised male who is not circumcised in the flesh of his foreskin shall be cut off from his people; he has broken my covenant."

Circumcision and the Sacrament of Baptism

Circumcision was "established as a rite by God under the Old Covenant."[38] It was a mark on a male and a sign that he was in covenant with God, sanctified for divine service and a member of the Jewish people.[39] The rite was performed on the eighth day after birth. It traditionally took place at home and was accompanied by prayers and naming the child. Today, circumcision is still an important ritual observed and celebrated with family and friends in the traditional Jewish community.[40]

In the Christian Church and under the New Covenant, circumcision is not a religious ritual. Paul wrote in Galatians 5: 6, "For in Christ Jesus, neither circumcision nor uncircumcision counts for anything, but only faith working through love." The Gentiles were not required to be circumcised because those who were uncircumcised according to Ephesians 2: 12-13, "were at one time without Christ... and strangers to the covenants of promise, having no hope and without God in the world. But now in Christ Jesus, you who once were far off have been **brought near by the blood of Christ**."

The ritual of circumcision does have similarities to the *Sacrament of Baptism*. Both traditionally involve a ceremony or ritual celebrated in the presence of family and friends plus a Godmother and a Godfather. For the Jewish faith, circumcision is a sign one belongs to God; whereas for the Christian, baptism is a sign one belongs to Christ. Circumcision incorporates one into the Jewish people while according to the Catechism of the Catholic Church, baptism incorporates one into the Church.[41] Unlike circumcision, The Catechism of the Catholic Church points out:

"Baptism is a reality that includes forgiveness of original sin and all personal sins, birth into the new life by which man becomes an adoptive son of the father, a member of Christ and a temple of the Holy Spirit."[42] Circumcision is an outward sign, while "baptism imprints on the soul an indelible spiritual sign, the character, which consecrates the baptized person for Christian worship."[43]

The Neighbors and Relatives Tried to Name Him Zechariah

Zechariah and Elizabeth's relatives and neighbors played a big part in their family's life. Here we see them helping name the baby whom they presume will be named after his father Zechariah. At that time, it was customary to name a first-born child after his grandfather to avoid confusion in calling father and son by the same name. However, this case was an exception; the child was a miracle. The neighbors probably thought Zechariah was old enough to be the grandfather anyway. When Elizabeth said "no" to naming the baby "Zechariah," they had to ask his father. Most certainly, they thought old Elizabeth must have been wrong in suggesting a name other than a family name.

5. **_ZECHARIAH SPEAKS._** (a) When the neighbors asked Zechariah about the baby's name, how did he respond (v. 61-63)? (b) Why do you think Zechariah was able to speak <u>only after</u> naming the baby _John_? (_Hint:_ See Luke 1: 20.) (c)What do you think Zechariah learned from his nine-month silent retreat when he was rendered mute? (d) What else happened as a result of Zechariah's tongue-loosed" miracle at John's circumcision (v. 65-66)?

_____

_____

_____

_____

_____

_____

_____

_____

Zechariah's Tongue is Freed

The Scriptures say, "**Immediately his mouth was opened and his tongue freed**" (v. 63). This happened as soon as Zechariah had fulfilled all that Angel Gabriel had commanded, including naming the baby "John." St Ambrose writes, "With good reason was his tongue loosed, because faith untied what had been tied by disbelief." [44]

The last words out of Zechariah's mouth were words of doubt. Now, we read that the next words out of Zechariah's mouth were words of praise to God. The nine months of silence had given him lots of time to ponder the closeness, the mercy and faithfulness of God. How could Zechariah, "filled with the Holy Spirit," help but praise God for all his marvelous works and faithfulness to Israel, to Elizabeth, to himself and to their new family?

6. _ZECHARIAH PRAISES GOD._ Read Luke 1: 67-80. (a) What were Zechariah's first words after being mute for nine months? (b) Circle the prophetic message about John and underline the prophetic message about Jesus ("Dawn from on High"). Share your thoughts.

_____

_____

_____

_____

_____

_____

_____

_____

_____

Luke 1: 67 - 80

Then his father Zechariah was filled with the Holy Spirit and spoke this prophecy:

> "Blessed be the Lord God of Israel, for he has looked favorably on his people and redeemed them. [69] He has raised up a mighty savior for us in the house of his servant David, [70] as he spoke through the mouth of his holy prophets from of old, [71] that we would be saved from our enemies and from the hand of all who hate us. [72] Thus he has shown the mercy promised to our ancestors, and has remembered his holy covenant, [73] the oath that he swore to our ancestor Abraham, to grant us [74] that we, being rescued from the hands of our enemies, might serve him without fear, [75] in holiness and righteousness before him all our days. [76] And you, child, will be called the prophet of the Most High; for you will go before the Lord to prepare his ways, [77] to give knowledge of salvation to his people by the forgiveness of their sins. [78] By the tender mercy of our God, the _dawn from on high_ will break upon us, [79] to give light to those who sit in darkness and in the shadow of death, to guide our feet into the way of peace." [80] The child grew and became strong in spirit, and he was in the wilderness until the day he appeared publicly to Israel.

Note: _**Dawn from on High**_ has also been translated "Rising Sun." NRSVCE

"Blessed Be"- The Benedictus Canticle

Zechariah's prophecy like Mary's Magnificat in Luke 1: 46-56 is called a *canticle.* **The word canticle** comes from the Latin term *"canticulum,"* which is translated "little song" and today, is used to describe liturgical songs taken from the Bible.[45]

The first word of Zechariah's canticle (v. 68) in St. Jerome's Latin translation of the Bible is *Benedictus* which means **"blessed be."** At this time in history, a priest on duty in the temple would leave the *Holy Place* after offering sacrifices and prayers for the nation and then come outside to the people, who were prayerfully waiting for him to bless them. In Luke 1:22, we read that Zechariah skipped the blessing because of his SHOCK from Gabriel's heavenly message and his sudden muteness. Now, nine months later and after obeying the words of God via Gabriel, Zechariah was ready to bless the Lord and his people.

The English word "benediction," a derivative of the word "Benedictus," means "invocation of a blessing in public worship."[46] The *Benedictus* canticle is sung every morning in the *Liturgy of the Hours* and is often said over the grave when a loved one is committed to God and the earth. [47]

7. THE THEMES OF THE BENEDICTUS. To reflect on the Benedictus, fill in the chart below with the basic themes and promises noted in Luke 1: 68-79.

Themes of the Benedictus – Luke 1: 68 - 79

Parts	Topics	Luke	Themes &Promises
Part 1: Praises	God fulfills OT promises – Savior in - King David Lineage - Covenant given to Abraham	v. 68 – 75	
Part 2: Prophecies-John	The Ministry of John the Baptist	v. 76-77	
Prophecies - Jesus	Jesus the Messiah (Dawn from on High)	v. 78-79	

Old Testament Prophecies Fulfilled

In the *Benedictus* canticle, Zechariah praised God that ancient (Old Testament) prophecies were being fulfilled. The promises fulfilled in Jesus include, 1) An offspring of David (ancestral line) will rule forever (2 Sam 7: 13-14), and 2) God hears His people's crying and remembers His covenant with Abraham to save them from their foes (Genesis 22: 16-17; Exodus 2: 24; Ezekiel 36: 28).

In some Bible translations, including the lectionary NABRE, **Mighty Savior** (v. 69) is translated "<u>**Horn** for our salvation.</u>" Horn for salvation is an Old Testament metaphor for the strength and power of God. (A horn refers to the strength of an ox or a horn found on a military helmet). Thus, Jesus would be our "**mighty savior**," who comes in the full strength of God (Ps. 18:3).

In Luke 1: 78, **"the Dawn from on High"** (NRSVCE) is also translated **"Rising Sun"** (Inclusive NT) or **Daybreak from on High"** (NABRE). These same terms, also found in Jeremiah 23: 5, Zechariah 3:8 and 6:12, are messianic titles for Jesus. "Daybreak from on High" (Rising Sun) means Jesus "breaks the darkness of sin and brings the daylight of God's forgiveness and peace."[48]

Zechariah prophesies that **John** will "go before the Lord to prepare his way (v. 76)" and the Savior (*Dawn from on High, Rising Sun*) will "gives light to those who sit in darkness." Jesus fulfilled this prophecy. In John 8:12, Jesus said: "I am the light of the world, he who follows me will not walk in darkness." The Bible tells us that Jesus is "the true light that enlightens every man" (John 1:9) and when we follow Him, we too become "the light of the world" (Matthew 5:14).

"[T]hose who sit in darkness and in the shadow of the earth" (v. 79) is explained by John Paul II when he quoted St. Bede on the Benedictus:

"Humanity that was engulfed in darkness and in the shadow of death is illumined by this dazzling revelation [of Christ] ...Thus, it is the Lord who comes to heal our blindness of sin and direct our steps 'to enable us to enter the home of eternal peace, which He has promised us.'"[49]

8. _MEDITATION ON THE FORERUNNER._ (a) To understand Zechariah's prophecy, read the following verses and <u>underline</u>

(*i*) John's purpose (Mark 1: 2),

(*ii*) John's message (Mark 1:3) and

(*iii*) The prophecies John would fulfill (Mark 1: 4-8, Luke 1: 76-77).

(b) Try to put yourself in the scene as you join the neighbors and relatives at the circumcision and naming. How would you describe the experience?

_____
_____
_____
_____
_____

Mark 1: 2-8. As it is written in Isaiah the prophet: "Behold, I am sending my messenger ahead of you; he will prepare your way. ³A voice of one crying out in the desert: 'Prepare the way of the Lord, make straight his paths.'" ⁴John [the] Baptist appeared in the desert proclaiming a baptism of repentance for the forgiveness of sins. ⁵People of the whole Judean countryside and all the inhabitants of Jerusalem were going out to him and were being baptized by him in the Jordan River as they acknowledged their sins. ⁶John was clothed in camel's hair, with a leather belt around his waist. He fed on locusts and wild honey. ⁷And this is what he proclaimed: "One mightier than I is coming after me. I am not worthy to stoop and loosen the thongs of his sandals. ⁸I have baptized you with water; he will baptize you with the holy Spirit."

Luke 1: 76-77. [Zechariah prophesied] "And you, child, will be called prophet of the Most High, for you will go before the Lord to prepare his ways, to give his people knowledge of salvation through the forgiveness of their sins." (a) Would you be shocked when Zechariah spoke and said the baby would be called John? (b) Are you finding silence (e.g., away from crowds, cell phones, politics, etc.) to ponder Jesus in His Holy Word so you can grow in faith— remember the silent retreat that helped Zechariah find faith again? (c) Are you singing the praises of God daily as Zechariah did— he pondered God's Word and saw surprising answers to prayer? (d) Try to pray the Benedictus often, especially during Advent as you prepare to celebrate His first coming? It is the same Jesus, who wants to be close to your heart now. He is the giver of Eternal Life and will come again as the King of Kings and Lord of Lords.

The Herald Had Come, but the Powerful Knew Nothing

Now that John the forerunner and herald had been born, the birth of the Savior was soon to follow. How like God that at the very time when the greatest event in the whole of creation was about to happen, very few knew about it. Abbott Fr. Gieuseppe Ricciotti (1947) once noted how interesting it was that the most powerful at the time — in and around Israel, were not aware of the monumental events happening on God's calendar:

> "God was NOT seeking the aid of the powerful in order to accomplish his plan of salvation, but the unknown, those hidden from the public view, the lowly like Zachary, Elizabeth, and Mary."[50]

Does it surprise you then, that often the ways of this world and the powerful are not the ways of God? It shouldn't! God works through his faithful ones who are often ridiculed and scorned by unbelievers. He works through average people and families, and the lowly and humble who seek Him, like you and me.

9. PERSONAL PRAYER RESPONSE. Write a prayer in response to what God spoke to you about Zechariah, John the Baptist and the Benedictus from this Chapter. Ask Jesus to help you reflect on the beautiful words of the Benedictus and the promises of Scripture concerning His coming and the Benedictus.

_____

_____

_____

_____

_____

_____

_____

_____

_____

_____

PRAYER EXAMPLE

Dear Jesus.

I bless your name, My Lord and My Savior.

Thank you for fulfilling your promises in Scripture.

Thank you for sending the forerunner John to proclaim your coming and prepare your people.

Thank you, Jesus, for redeeming us and forgiving our sins. You shed your blood and died on the cross for us...for me.

Thank you for delivering me from my enemies, for your mercy and for your faithfulness.

Dear Lord, I commit my life and my family to you.

Please open the eyes of all my family to faith. I pray that the "hearts of parents will turn to their children" and "the hearts of children to their parents."

Call my children to be heralds of the Good News and bring others to YOU.

And I pray the **Benedictus**:

The Benedictus

Blessed be the Lord, the God of Israel;
He has come to His people and set them free.
He has raised up for us a mighty savior,
born of the house of His servant David.

Through His holy prophets He promised of old
that He would save us from our enemies,
from the hands of all who hate us.

He promised to show mercy to our fathers
And to remember His holy covenant.
This was the oath he swore to our father Abraham:
to set us free from the hands of our enemies,
free to worship Him without fear,
holy and righteous in His sight
all the days of our life.

You, my child, shall be called the prophet
of the Most High;
for you will go before the Lord to prepare His way,
to give His people knowledge of salvation
by the forgiveness of their sins.

In the tender compassion of our God
the *Dawn from on High* shall break upon us,
to shine on those who dwell in darkness
and the shadow of death,
and to guide our feet into the way of peace.

Glory to the Father, and to the Son,
and to the Holy Spirit,
as it was in the beginning, is now,
and will be forever. Amen.

5

Joseph Takes Mary for His Wife

Connection Question

What do you know about your own ancestry?
Is there anyone in your family tree who embarrasses you?

The Dream of St. Joseph[51]
by Anton Raphael Mengs, 1773
United States Public Domain

Chapter Five - Joseph Takes Mary for His Wife

Old Testament Prophecies Fulfilled

Our journey chronologically leads us next from Luke's Gospel to Matthew's Gospel. Matthew fills us in on important details about Mary's return home from Zechariah and Elizabeth's home and her betrothed Joseph. Matthew originally wrote his Gospel to a predominantly Jewish audience and thus, made special effort to establish that Jesus descended from Abraham, the Father of Israel, and from David, the King of Israel. Purity of blood lineage and fulfillment of Old Testament prophecies were very important to the faithful Israelites who were awaiting the Messiah's coming.

Matthew begins his account with a genealogy. Jesus' kingly ancestry would prove that He was the one who fulfilled Old Testament prophecies, such as "The scepter shall never depart from Judah" (Genesis 49:10) and "Never shall David lack a successor on the throne" (Jeremiah 33:14-17). Interestingly, we will see that Jesus' ancestry includes some not-so-saintly members too!

Chapter Five Questions

1. THE GENEALOGY OF JESUS. Read Matthew 1: 1-17 and list the four female and "not-so-saintly" members in Jesus' genealogy. Share your thoughts.

_____
_____
_____
_____
_____
_____
_____
_____
_____
_____

Matthew 1: 1-17

[1] An account of the genealogy of Jesus the Messiah, the son of David, the son of Abraham. [2] Abraham was the father of Isaac, and Isaac the father of Jacob, and Jacob the father of Judah and his brothers, [3]and Judah the father of Perez and Zerah by Tamar, and Perez the father of Hezron, and Hezron the father of Aram, [4] and Aram the father of Aminadab, and Aminadab the father of Nahshon, and Nahshon the father of Salmon, [5] and Salmon the father of Boaz by Rahab, and Boaz the father of Obed by Ruth, and Obed the father of Jesse, [6] and Jesse the father of King David.

And David was the father of Solomon by the wife of Uriah, [7] and Solomon the father of Rehoboam, and Rehoboam the father of Abijah, and Abijah the father of Asaph, [8] and Asaph the father of Jehoshaphat, and Jehoshaphat the father of Joram, and Joram the father of Uzziah, [9] and Uzziah the father of Jotham, and Jotham the father of Ahaz, and Ahaz the father of Hezekiah, [10] and Hezekiah the father of Manasseh, and Manasseh the father of Amos, and Amos the father of Josiah, [11] and Josiah the father of Jechoniah and his brothers, at the time of the deportation to Babylon.

[12] And after the deportation to Babylon: Jechoniah was the father of Salathiel, and Salathiel the father of Zerubbabel, [13] and Zerubbabel the father of Abiud, and Abiud the father of Eliakim, and Eliakim the father of Azor, [14] and Azor the father of Zadok, and Zadok the father of Achim, and Achim the father of Eliud, [15] and Eliud the father of Eleazar, and Eleazar the father of Matthan, and Matthan the father of Jacob, [16] and Jacob the father of Joseph the husband of Mary, of whom Jesus was born, who is called the Messiah.[17] So all the generations from Abraham to David are fourteen generations; and from David to the deportation to Babylon, fourteen generations; and from the deportation to Babylon to the Messiah, fourteen generations.

2. *THE PATRIARCHS.* According to Matthew1: 1-6 and 16, how is Jesus related to the patriarchs of faith?

_____

_____

_____

_____

_____

_____

_____

_____

_____

The Family Record

At the time of Jesus, families kept a genealogical record (family tree) for use in the distribution of inherited property and other rights under Jewish laws. Even though Jesus was the adopted son of Joseph, God had a plan that the Jewish people would be able to trace His family tree back to Abraham, the Father of Israel and to David, the King of Israel.

The genealogy of Jesus presented in Matthew 1 is more a family record than a perfect historical account that might include every member in the ancestry of Jesus Christ as Messiah. As Pope Benedict XVI pointed out, "that was not Matthew's goal."[52] Instead, Matthew wrote to appeal to the Jews by placing Jesus first and foremost as the Son of Abraham—the Patriarch and Father of Israel promised as part of an everlasting covenant with God (Genesis 17: 6-7), and as the Son of David—the priestly King of Israel, whose ancestors were prophesied to reign forever (2 Samuel: 7:13). Matthew's genealogy ends with Mary (Matthew 1: 16) which points to a new beginning in the record. Jesus was not conceived by man but "through the Holy Spirit" (Matthew 1: 20). Joseph is the legal father, but God is truly the Father.[53]

You will notice that the names in Matthew's genealogy are grouped into three sets of fourteen generations centered on King David: "Abraham to David are fourteen generations; and from David to the deportation to Babylon, fourteen generations; and from the deportation to Babylon to the Messiah, fourteen generations" (Matthew 1:17). Since the Hebrew letters in David's name add up to fourteen, Pope Benedict says, this genealogy truly proclaims, "the Gospel of Christ the King" with the whole of history looking "toward him whose throne is to endure forever."[54]

Interestingly, Luke 3: 23-38 provides us with another genealogy, but it does not appear until the beginning of Jesus's public ministry. Luke offers a family record of Christ's genealogy, covering 77 generations and starting backwards from Jesus, including David, Noah, Adam and ending with God. Luke's goals is different from Matthew's as Luke points out he "continuity of God's action in history" and that Jesus truly is the Savior of the World. He is indicating that "humanity starts afresh in Jesus."[55] Luke and Matthew are different in covering Jesus' ancestry because Matthew presents Joseph's point of view (e.g., his dreams and decisions) and Luke presents Mary's (e.g., the annunciation, her relatives Elizabeth and Zechariah.) Whereas Matthew emphasizes Jesus' kingly heritage, Luke emphasized his priestly heritage.[56]

3. *FOREIGNERS, ADULTERERS, & PROSTITUTES.* Fill in the blanks in the following chart after you read about the lives of each woman listed in Matthew 1. You will need to use your own Bible to read more about these four women in Scripture.

The Four Women in the Lineage of Jesus Christ from Mathew

Woman's Name & Scriptures	Details of Her Life (From Your Bible)	How She Was Related to Christ
Tamar **Genesis 38: 1-30**	A Canaanite who played a prostitute to Judah, who refused to give his son in marriage after her first husband died as required by Jewish law; she was faithful to family and to God's law.	**Example.** She had a son by Jacob's son **Judah** and bore **Perez**, who was in the line of David and Christ.
Rahab **Joshua 2:1-24 and 6: 22-25**	A Canaanite prostitute of Jericho who risked her life to help Joshua's spies escape. She repented in deeds and converted to become an Israelite.	
Ruth **Ruth 1:1-18**	Moabitess pagan woman, non-Israelite, convert, faithful to her mother-in-law Naomi and to God's law.	
Bathsheba **2 Samuel 11 and Psalm 51***	A Hittite adulteress, who was seduced by the king, received God's judgment on her firstborn, and repented to receive a son named Solomon, who became King of Israel.	

Note: *Psalm 51 was written by David as a cry for mercy after he and Bathsheba committed adultery and she became pregnant. David had arranged for her husband Uriah to be killed. David repented of his terrible sins with Bathsheba. God forgave them.

Christ is Not Ashamed to Call Them Brethren

Jewish pedigrees at the time of Christ, usually did not contain names of women because women were regarded as assets of their husbands. Matthew's lineage of Christ interestingly includes four women. The women named in Matthew 1 were all recipients of God 's grace and mercy. Although Jesus had a kingly heritage, He was not ashamed of these women of foreign ancestry or prior immorality, who for those reasons might have been disqualified from inclusion in His kingly lineage.

Tamar, Rahab, Ruth, and Bathsheba were all Gentile women who <u>repented and became faithful to God</u> in their circumstances. Thus, the lineage in Mathew shows us that the Gospel message of forgiveness in Jesus Christ breaks down barriers between Jew and Gentile, male and female, saint and sinner. All people are important to God. <u>Jesus came for all who will come to Him</u>. He came to justify sinners, and to "all who received him, who believed in his name, he gave power to become children of God, who were born, not of blood or of the will of the flesh or of the will of man, but of God" (John 1: 12-13).

Today, He still comes for the sinners and the outcasts and for all who feel excluded from God's family. By mentioning outcasts and those of disrepute, Matthew reminds us that God's ways are different from our ways. The *Navarre Bible* points out:

> "God will sometimes carry out His plan of salvation by means of people whose conduct had not been just. God saves us, sanctifies us and chooses us to do good despite our sins and infidelities---and He chose to leave evidence of this at various stages in the history of our salvation."[57]

God's plan of salvation does not change, in spite of our sins. Jesus came to redeem us from the penalty of sin and to give us new life in Him. Even if your past life or your "family tree" is disreputable, Jesus will give you forgiveness, grace, mercy and a new beginning when you come to Him in faith and repentance. You are part of the family of God, and every day you can have new life in Christ. Hebrews 2: 11 reinforces this: "God is not ashamed to call them [or you] brothers and sisters." Peter said, "**Repent** therefore, <u>**turn to God so that your sins may be wiped out,**</u> so that times of refreshing may come from the presence of the Lord" (Acts 3:19).

Pope Benedict XVI writing on the deeper meaning of the genealogies of Jesus reinforces our true genealogy to be in Christ, our new origin:

> "[T]hose who believe in Jesus enter through faith into Jesus' unique new origin, and they receive this origin as their own...Jesus was not begotten by Joseph but was truly born of the Holy Spirit from the Virgin Mary, so it can now be said of us that our true 'genealogy' is faith in Jesus, who gives us a new origin, who brings us to birth 'from God'."[58]

4. _THE BIRTH OF JESUS._ Read Matthew 1: 18-25 and circle the words that indicate when Mary was "found with child." Share your thoughts.

_____
_____
_____
_____
_____
_____
_____
_____

Matthew 1: 18-25

Now the birth of Jesus the Messiah took place in this way. When his mother Mary had been engaged [betrothed] to Joseph, but before they lived together, she was found to be with child from the Holy Spirit. [19] Her husband Joseph, being a righteous man and unwilling to expose her to public disgrace, planned to dismiss her quietly. [20] But just when he had resolved to do this, an angel of the Lord appeared to him in a dream and said, "Joseph, son of David, do not be afraid to take Mary as your wife, for the child conceived in her is from the Holy Spirit. [21] She will bear a son, and you are to name him Jesus, for he will save his people from their sins." [22] All this took place to fulfill what had been spoken by the Lord through the prophet:

[23] "Look, the virgin shall conceive and bear a son, and they shall name him Emmanuel," which means, "God is with us." [24] When Joseph awoke from sleep, he did as the angel of the Lord commanded him; he took her as his wife, [25] but had no marital relations with her until she had borne a son; and he named him Jesus.

5. *FOUND WITH CHILD.* (a) What could it mean to Joseph and to the neighbors that Mary was found pregnant while they were betrothed (not yet married) (v. 19)? (b) What does v. 24-25 indicate about Joseph?

_____

_____

_____

_____

_____

_____

_____

Joseph

Mary returned home from visiting Elizabeth and Zechariah and was beginning to look pregnant. She would use some of the strength she received from Elizabeth to face any perceived humiliation, and the apparent rejection from those who did not know or would not believe that "a virgin was with child." Even Joseph knew the child was not his. Did he think Mary had broken the engagement? Did he find it incomprehensible or was he piously fearful?

Abbott Fr. Gieuseppe Ricciotti suggests: "He had not been forewarned of the supernatural conception...Did he perhaps think that while blameless herself, she had suffered some violence during those three months of absence?"[59] We don't know the details, because Matthew doesn't tell us. However, Matthew does inform us that Joseph could have given her a bill of divorce, under the existing law, which most certainly would result in public ridicule and "expose her to public disgrace" (v. 19). Instead, Joseph, a "righteous man," walking in love, sensitivity and justice with commitment to the Law of God, decided to "divorce her quietly" to protect her reputation. "But as he was resolved to do this" (v. 20), the Lord took care of his perplexity through a dream with an angel.

Note. Betrothed (NABRE) or engaged (NRSVCE) in Matthew 1: 18-19 was a cultural norm that involved a ceremony where two people made a commitment to marry. It was a legally binding contract like a marriage, but there would be no sexual intimacy until the couple moved in together about one year later. Joseph had decided to divorce Mary quietly. Legally, she could be stoned for committing adultery since she was "found with child" while betrothed to Joseph (Deuteronomy 22: 23-24). (See detailed explanation of betrothal in Chapter 3.)

6. *THE ANGEL OF THE LORD.* (a) Although the Bible does NOT say, who do you think appeared to Joseph in the dream (v. 20, 22)?(b) What would the words in the angel's greeting mean to Joseph (Consider what you know about the kingly lineage of Jesus from question #3)?

_____

_____

_____

_____

_____

_____

_____

Notes. **The angel of the Lord** (v. 20) was an Old Testament way of referring to God's visible presence among His people or saying that God was communicating with a human being.[60] Some think the dream may have included Gabriel.

Dreams were a common way that God communicated with His people in the Old Testament. In Numbers 12: 6, God said, "When there are prophets among you, I the Lord, make myself known to them; I speak to them in dreams." God used dreams in the New Testament to guide Joseph to flee to Egypt (Matthew 2:12-13), to tell Joseph to return to Galilee (Matthew 2:22), and to warn Pilate via his wife against harming Jesus (Matthew 27:19). Today, most of the time our dreams are not necessarily messages from God.

7. *A VIRGIN IS WITH CHILD*. (a) Read Isaiah 7:14 below and compare it to Mathew 1: 23. (b) What Old Testament prophecy given over 700 years in advance was to be fulfilled?

_____

_____

_____

_____

_____

_____

_____

Isaiah 7: 14. Therefore the Lord himself will give you a sign. Look, the young woman [virgin] is with child and shall bear a son and shall name him Immanuel.

Matthew 1: 23. "Look, the virgin shall conceive and bear a son, and they shall name him Emmanuel," which means, "God is with us."

"Name Him Jesus" and They Did

Both Mary and Joseph were given the name for the Christ Child. In a dream <u>and</u> in person, the angel told Mary and Joseph to name the baby "Jesus." Jesus means "Savior" and in Matthew 1: 21, the full meaning of the name is clearly spelled out, "because He will save his people from their sins." (See further meaning of the name Jesus in *Chapter 2, Jesus Named after His Heavenly Father*.)

Immanuel (sometimes spelled Emmanuel) means "God is with us" (v. 23), and Jesus is truly God-with-us, fulfilling the prophecy of Isaiah 7:14. Jesus, God in flesh (Incarnate), actually dwelt on earth bringing His presence to us. Jesus before His Ascension (Matthew 28: 20) said: "Behold, I am with you always, until the end of the age." Praise God, Jesus is always with you, now and forever.

8. JOSEPH'S RESPONSE. What did Joseph's response to the angel's message in the dream convey about his faith (v. 23-24)?

_____

_____

_____

_____

_____

_____

_____

_____

Joseph Responds Immediately

Joseph did not hesitate in his response to God; he trusted God to work everything out for good. He willingly exchanged his plans for God's plan. Joseph's neighbors may have gossiped, and his relatives may have wondered what happened to the year-long betrothal-engagement, but Joseph chose to obey and put his trust in God.

This was the beginning of Joseph's mission for life. One could say that Joseph was born for this vocation -- to be the father of Jesus and to be Mary's most chaste spouse. Fr. Francis Fernandez (1997) says, this is the "same way that every person who comes into the world has a specific vocation from God, in which is rooted the whole meaning of his life." Joseph said, "yes" to his vocation. He would be the head of the Holy family and his entire happiness was in understanding "what God wanted of him and in his having faithfully carried it out to the end."[61]

Once Joseph heard the message of God through the angel, he immediately obeyed and "took his wife into his home" (NABRE, v. 24). The friends and families and relatives may have come to a small celebration, but the profoundness of the mystery was hidden between God and the newlyweds. "And Joseph, from the tribe of Judah and the house of David, a carpenter by trade, became the legal head of that little family."[62] What a role model Joseph is to our families— in so many ways he displayed a heart totally given to God and not one that first seeks the approval of others, but yearns to love, cherish and protect his family.

9. REFLECTION ON THE LINEAGE OF CHRIST AND ST. JOSEPH. Now is a good time to reflect on St. Joseph, in the linage of David and chosen to be the husband of Mary and earthly father of Jesus. Can you picture the bewilderment of Joseph when plans did not go the way he thought they would or the sudden changes that came to his life? Consider the following applications.

(a) Like St. Joseph, are you open to changed plans that fit with God's plan? Talk to Jesus about what you can you do to stay open to God's plan?

_____

_____

_____

(b) Is your heart surrendered to Jesus or do you seek the approval of those who don't walk in God's ways? Talk to Jesus about his approval of you.

_____

_____

_____

(c) Are you willing to be God's adopted daughter or son? Romans 8: 14-15 reminds us that God adopts us in love: "For all who are led by the Spirit of God are the sons of God. For you did not receive the spirit of slavery leading again to fear, but you received the Spirit of adoption, by whom we cry, 'Abba, Father'." Talk to Jesus about being his daughter.

_____

_____

_____

10. MY PERSONAL PRAYER RESPONSE. Try to write a prayer focusing on your commitment to walk with Jesus, to be led by the Holy Spirit and to follow God's plan for your life. See the following example.

_____

_____

_____

PRAYER EXAMPLE

Dear Lord Jesus,

Thank you that you are my Immanuel—You are with me.   Thank you that you are merciful and forgiving to all who come to you.

Your lineage tells me that you are not ashamed to call sinners your "brothers and sisters" when they repent and follow you.

Thank you that my true 'genealogy' is faith in Jesus, and I have a new origin. Thank you for giving St. Joseph to your church as a model father and husband. Help me to respond in obedience to your message as Joseph did.

Thank you, dear Jesus, for coming to live in me and for dying to be my Savior.

Lord, I give you my heart. I give you my life.

6

Our Savior is Born, Shepherds Praise & Angels Sing

Connection Question

Did you ever move away from your hometown?
How did you feel when you left the town where you were raised?

The Adoration of the Shepherds[63]
by Domenico Zampieri, 1607-1610
United States Public Domain[64]

Chapter Six - Our Savior is Born

Shepherds Praise & Angel's Sing

The Journey to Bethlehem

It's time for the birth of our Savior. So now we return to Luke's Gospel since Matthew 2 covers only the events that occur directly after Jesus' birth. We will join Mary and Joseph on their 80-mile journey to Bethlehem. The walking and riding would be very difficult and uncomfortable for Mary who is nine-months pregnant. The roads would be busy with caravans of foot travelers, camels, and donkeys. A journey of eighty miles would usually take four days, so both Mary and Joseph must endure stopping overnight at public inns, staying with relatives or friends when possible, or even sleeping on the ground with the caravan and animals.[65] Finally, they will arrive in Jerusalem to find it crowded with people, who, like Mary and Joseph, had come at the command of Caesar Augustus for the census.

Chapter Six Questions

1. FROM NAZARETH TO BETHLEHEM. Read Luke 2: 1-20 and any words the relate to the political and legal reasons why Joseph had to go to Bethlehem. Share your thoughts.

_____

_____

_____

_____

_____

_____

_____

_____

_____

Luke 2: 1-7

In those days, a decree went out from Emperor Augustus that all the world should be registered. 2 This was the first registration and was taken while Quirinius was governor of Syria. 3 All went to their own towns to be registered. 4 Joseph also went from the town of Nazareth in Galilee to Judea, to the city of David called Bethlehem, because he was descended from the house and family of David. 5 He went to be registered with Mary, to whom he was engaged and who was expecting a child. 6 While they were there, the time came for her to deliver her child. 7And she gave birth to her firstborn son and wrapped him in bands of cloth, and laid him in a manger, because there was no place for them in the inn.

> **Note. Caesar Augustus** was emperor of Rome from 27 BC to 14 AD. His real name was Octavian. The title *Caesar* was taken from the family name of Julius Caesar, Father of the Roman Empire. He chose the name Augustus, which means "most reverent one."

2. BETHLEHEM. (a) What is the prophetic reason for Joseph going to Bethlehem as recorded in Micah 1: 3? (b) Why do you think Joseph took Mary with him when she was 9 months pregnant?

_____

_____

_____

_____

_____

_____

_____

_____

_____

Micah 5:1-3. But you, Bethlehem-Ephrathah, too small to be among the clans of Judah, from you shall come forth for me one who is to be ruler in Israel; whose origin is from of old, from ancient times. Therefore, the Lord will give them up until the time when she who is to give birth has born...He shall stand firm and shepherd His flock by the strength of the Lord in the majestic name of the Lord His God..." NRSVCE

Jesus Would Be Born in Bethlehem

Jesus would be born in Bethlehem, in the City of David, in the lineage of David. His birth in Bethlehem would fulfill the words prophesied by the prophet Micah over 700 years earlier. Roman Emperor Caesar Augustus, a master bookkeeper and statistician, probably knew nothing of the prophecy but it was his policy to carefully keep track of his subjects and his kingdom by public enrollment.[66] As any ruler knew, a census would aid in taxation and military conscription, so Caesar Augustus issued his decree.

Caesar's decree required people to register in the town of their ancestral origin so Joseph would have to go to Bethlehem, as he was a descendent of King David. Mary may have gone on the journey because as a descendant of Judah, she too was required to register – women were not always required to register, but in some geographical regions, women were included in the decree. OR Mary may have gone with Joseph because her delivery was so near that Joseph did not want to leave her alone. OR Mary and Joseph were considering moving near Jerusalem anyway. After all, Gabriel told them that Jesus would be given the throne of David, and they knew that the *House of David* originated in Jerusalem.[67]

3. BORN IN A STABLE. What imagery does Luke 2: 7 bring to mind when you consider the Lord of all creation was born in a stable and slept in an animal's food trough for his bed?

_____
_____
_____
_____
_____
_____
_____
_____
_____
—

The Stable and the First Born

The *stable* was a place where the animals were fed from a manger or feeding trough. Stables, at that time, were often small caves carved in a rock or hill near a village or inn. They were usually dark and dirty. At least, there would be a fresh bed of straw and privacy for the expectant mother. There in the seclusion of the stable, in humility and lowliness, Jesus was born, and the Holy Family came into being. Mary "wrapped him in swaddling clothes and laid him in a manger."

The *swaddling clothes* were bands of cloths that mothers used and still use in the Mideast to tightly wrap babies and give them warmth and security. The idea of swaddling clothes could be compared somewhat to the baby wraps that new mothers use today to carry their infants on their bodies. It would have a similar effect.

You may notice that Jesus was called the "First-Born Son" (v. 7). According to St. Jerome, "Every only-begotten is a *first born*, though not every first born is an *only* son. First-born does not mean him after whom came others, but him *before whom no child is born.*"[68]

> **Note. Swaddling clothes,** based on tradition, were used to wrap newly born lambs that were without blemish and could be used in temple sacrifice.[69] These sacrificial lambs would be wrapped to preserve their purity as required by law and then placed in a food trough apart from the other sheep. Thus, the sight of Jesus wrapped in swaddling *clothes* was truly a sign that Jesus was born to be a sacrificial lamb for our sins.

4. THE INN. Why do you think God allowed there to be "no room in the inn" for the Holy Family and His soon-to-be-born only begotten son?

_____

_____

_____

_____

_____

_____

_____

No Home for the Creator of Creation

Joseph tried to find housing for Mary and the baby in her womb, but Bethlehem and Jerusalem were too crowded with thousands of pilgrims coming for the census registration. He probably tried the homes of relatives or friends as well as public inns, but no place of privacy was available—all were full. Most Reverend Fulton J. Sheen pointed out: "He searched in vain for a place where He, to Whom heaven and earth belonged, might be born. Could it be that the Creator would not find a home in creation?"[70] Bishop Sheen explained why the God of all creation would have been born in the smelly filth of a stable and then put to bed in a trough where animals ate:

The inn is the gathering place of public opinion, the focal point of the world's moods, the rendezvous of the worldly, the rallying place of the popular and the successful. But the stable is a place for the outcasts, the ignored, the forgotten. The world might have expected the Son of God to be born—if He was to be born at all—in an inn. A stable would be the last place in the world where one would have looked for Him. **Divinity is always where one least expects to find it**.[71]

In a crowded, busy life, the manger scene reminds us that God can be missed, and that doing God's will often takes us out of our comfort zones. Spiritually-speaking, our hearts can be the open inn where Jesus is born and lives in us and through us. The Navarre Commentary says, "Our hearts should provide Jesus with a place where he can be born spiritually, that is we should be born in a new life, becoming a new creature (Romans 6: 4), keeping that holiness and purity of soul which, we were given in Baptism and which is like being born again."[72]

The Fields Outside of Bethlehem

Although we wanted to pause with Mary and Joseph and celebrate the birth of our Savior, Luke doesn't let us tarry long. Only a few hours of nighttime passed when Luke leads us from the manger to the fields outside of Bethlehem. There we find an unassuming group, wide awake, yes, in the middle of the night, because their vocation requires such vigilance. So, we are "off" to see who they are and why they are such an important part in the birth of Christ.

5. _GOOD TIDINGS OF GREAT JOY._ (a) Read Luke 2: 8-20 and circle every reference to the shepherds and all with them. (b)Who were the first ones to hear the announcement of the Savior's birth? Why would the Lord choose these ones to be first? (c) Although no name was mentioned, who do you think the angel was?

_____
_____
_____
_____
_____
_____
_____

Luke 2: 8-20

8 In that region there were shepherds living in the fields, keeping watch over their flock by night. 9 Then an angel of the Lord stood before them, and the glory of the Lord shone around them, and they were terrified. 10 But the angel said to them, "Do not be afraid; for see — I am bringing you good news of great joy for all the people: 11 to you is born this day in the city of David a Savior, who is the Messiah, the Lord. 12 This will be a sign for you: you will find a child wrapped in bands of cloth and lying in a manger." 13 And suddenly there was with the angel a multitude of the heavenly host, praising God and saying, 14 "Glory to God in the highest heaven, and on earth peace among those whom he favors!"

15 When the angels had left them and gone into heaven, the shepherds said to one another, "Let us go now to Bethlehem and see this thing that has taken place, which the Lord has made known to us." 16 So they went with haste and found Mary and Joseph, and the child lying in the manger. 17 When they saw this, they made known what had been told them about this child; 18 and all who heard it were amazed at what the shepherds told them. 19 But Mary treasured all these words and pondered them in her heart. 20 The shepherds returned, glorifying and praising God for all they had heard and seen, as it had been told them.

The Shepherds and the Angels

The shepherds in our modern nativity scenes may be a somewhat embellished picture of those who responded to the angel's message and sought out the Messiah. Shepherds guarded sheep in all kinds of weather, lived a nomadic life with few conveniences and were probably stinky, dirty, and rough, to say the least. They carried clubs to gash the heads of wolves or other animals that threatened their sheep. Often the youngest boy in a family, once he was old enough to withstand the cold nights and could run fairly fast, was assigned the job (the older children took on the farming chores). Here is the important lesson from the shepherds for us: lowly, plain, ordinary folks, outcasts, and those of little value in the eyes of the world, like the shepherds, are the ones the Lord chose to herald his coming.

The shepherds couldn't miss the Glory of the Lord and how magnificent it was! The glory shown all around the shepherds. The purest light shines even brighter in the darkness of night.

6. _THE SHEPHERDS AND THE SIGN._ (a) What sign did the angel promise the shepherds (Luke 2: 12)? (b) According to Ezekiel 34: 11-16 and Psalm 23: 1-4, how does God relate to shepherds and sheep?

_____

_____

_____

_____

_____

_____

_____

_____

Ezekiel 34: 11-16. For thus says the Lord God: I myself will search for my sheep and will seek them out... I will rescue them from all the places to which they have been scattered on a day of clouds and thick darkness. ... 14 I will feed them with good pasture... 15 I myself will be the shepherd of my sheep, and I will make them lie down, says the Lord God. 16 I will seek the lost, and I will bring back the strayed, and I will bind up the injured, and I will strengthen the weak, but the fat and the strong I will destroy. I will feed them with justice. NRSVCE

Psalm 23: 1-4. The Lord is my shepherd, I shall not want. 2 He makes me lie down in green pastures; he leads me beside still waters; 3 he restores my soul. He leads me in right paths for his name's sake. 4 Even though I walk through the darkest valley, I fear no evil; for you are with me; your rod and your staff—they comfort me.

Note: The Sign. An angel told the shepherds that there would be <u>a sign</u> for them (v. 12), "a child wrapped in swaddling clothes and lying in a manger." The word "sign" in New Testament Greek is *"semeion"* and it refers to a miraculous event, a supernatural wonder, or the very touch of God's hand."[73] The sign of "the infant wrapped in swaddling clothes and lying in a manger" (v. 12) and found by the shepherds was truly a sign of God touching earth. God was authenticating the birth of His only son—it was a miraculous event—the God of heaven came to dwell with us and he came as a sacrificial lamb (see the note on *swaddling clothes* under *Stable and First Born*).

Light Shines in the Darkness

It is not only amazing that God chooses shepherds—the little, the lowly, the despised of the world (1 Corinthians 1: 28), but that he also calls himself a shepherd (e.g., "I am the Good Shepherd," John 10:11). The Lord describes himself as one who "shepherds rightly:" he tends sheep, rescues them, leads them, gives them rest, brings back the lost, binds up the injured, heals the sick, but destroys the sleek (Ezekiel 34:12-16).

If Jesus says He is our shepherd, then that means God Almighty chooses the humble of the world. God planned the key event in the history of mankind to happen in silence, where the powerful of the world hardly noticed. The glory of the Lord shines brightest in the darkness of the night watch. Who could miss it? The shepherds couldn't for they had been chosen to be the first to hear the good news, "For today in the city of David a Savior has been born for you who is Messiah, the Lord" (Luke 2: 11).

If at times you feel "lowly" or you think you are the lowliest among others. Please know that Christ is YOUR Savior and Shepherd. He came for you! You are His little lamb, and He loves you.

<u>7. The Angel's Gloria.</u> (a) Read Luke 2: 10-14 and describe the **angel's message to the shepherds in** v. 10-11. (b) **Who** ultimately are the recipients of the message (v. 10-11)? (c) **What emotion** comes to the recipients when they hear the Good News (v. 10)? (d) Who joined the angel of the Lord and what did they say (v. 13)?

_____

_____

_____

_____

_____

_____

Luke 2: 10-14

10 But the angel said to them, "Do not be afraid; for see—I am bringing you good news of great joy for all the people: 11 to you is born this day in the city of David a Savior, who is the Messiah, the Lord. 12 This will be a sign for you: you will find a child wrapped in bands of cloth and lying in a manger." 13 And suddenly there was with the angel a multitude of the heavenly host, praising God and saying, 14 "Glory to God in the highest heaven, and on earth peace among those whom he favors!"

The Gloria - the Angel's Song of Praise

The *Angel's Song* is a canticle of praise to God and has become known as the "Gloria" because the first word in St. Jerome's Latin translation of Luke 2: 14 is "Gloria." The continual adoration and worship by the angels surrounding our Lord is joined by His Church on earth, praising and singing to Him.   The Catechism of the Catholic Church explains:

"From the Incarnation to the Ascension, the life of the Word incarnate is surrounded by the adoration and service of angels. When God brings the firstborn in to the world, he says; 'Let all God's angels worship him.' Their song of praise at the birth of Christ has not ceased resounding in the Church's praise: 'Glory to God in the Highest!' They protect Jesus in his infancy, serve him in the desert, strengthen him in his agony in the garden, when he could have been saved by them from the hands of his enemies as Israel had been. Again, it is the angels who 'evangelize' by proclaiming the Good News of Christ's Incarnation and Resurrection. They will be present at Christ's return, which they will announce, to serve at his judgment."[74]

The angels sing because Christ is their Lord and thus, they adore him. St. Gregory the Great says, they put "the notes of their hymn in harmony with our redemption; they see us as already sharing in their own happy destiny and rejoice at this."[75]

8. THE FIRST EVANGELIZERS. (a) Read Luke 2: 15-20 and share who were the first evangelizers/ proclaimers of the Good News (v. 17, 18 and 20). (b) Why were the shepherds so joy-filled? (c) How did the listeners respond to the Shepherd's message (v.18)? (d) How did Mary respond to the Shepherd's message (v. 18-19)?

_____

_____

_____

_____

The Good News: Jesus is Savior, Messiah and Lord

The angel's message of "Good News" in Luke 2:10-14 is summarized in the announcement: "To you is born this day in the city of David a **Savior**, who is the **Messiah**, the **Lord**." It is important to note these titles:

Savior is *Soter* in New Testament Greek and means *God Saves*. Thus, the Catechism of the Catholic Church points out: Jesus is the ONE "who saves His people from their sins," and from eternal death.[76]

Messiah is *Christos* in New Testament Greek or *Christ* in English and literally means *Anointed One*. In the Old Testament, anointings were reserved for kings, priests, and prophets—those "consecrated to God for a mission" (Leviticus 4: 5). Thus, the title Messiah had special meaning to the Jewish people. They were expecting an anointed king to emerge from the line of David and inaugurate God's kingdom on earth (2 Samuel 7: 13-14). The Catechism of the Catholic Church says, Jesus is "anointed by the Spirit of the Lord at once as king and priest and also as prophet," and He was sent by God to "inaugurate His kingdom definitively."[77]

Lord, *Kyrios* in New Testament Greek or *Yahweh* in Hebrew, means master or sovereign. The Catechism of the Catholic Church says, "The New Testament uses the title **Lord** both for the Father and—what is new—**for Jesus**, who is thereby recognized as God Himself.[78] The title "Lord" asserts that the "power, honor, and glory due to God the Father are due also to Jesus," and He is divinely sovereign.[79]

Therefore, we can say with assurance:

Jesus is our Savior, who delivers us from sin and alienation from God.

Jesus is our Messiah, the Anointed One, who will reign forever and ever throughout all eternity.

Jesus is our Lord, who as God Himself, is divinely sovereign and has and will have dominion over all.

**9. MARY PONDERED.** (a) What do you think Mary treasured or pondered in her heart (v.19)? (b) Consider what the Angel said, what Elizabeth said, what Joseph said, and what the shepherds said that would inspire Mary.

_____

_____

_____

_____

_____

_____

_____

_____

Mary Treasured and Pondered God's Words

One insight we learn about Mary and the fact she "treasured and pondered" these things in her heart is that Mary was likely Luke's source for this information.[80] Mary kept pondering and reflecting on all the events that had happened and the words God sent to her. Can you imagine her thoughts of the shepherds, who spoke about a message from an angel and a singing heavenly host of angels (v. 12)? Can you imagine what she thought as she reflected on Gabriel and his message about the Baby she now held in her arms?

Mary stands as an example for us in treasuring, pondering, meditating on and delighting in the things God has revealed to us, especially since we have the Word of God in Scripture. Psalm 1: 1-2 tells us this: "Happy are those who do not follow the advice of the wicked, or take the path that sinners tread, or sit in the seat of scoffers; but their delight is in the law of the Lord, and on his law, they meditate day and night." This is especially important when, like Mary, we do not fully understand or know what lies ahead. We can trust in God, His faithfulness and His Word to keep us.

10. REFLECTION ON THE BIRTH OF JESUS. This is a good time to reflect on the details surrounding the Birth of Jesus. Try to put yourself in the scenes—traveling with Mary and Joseph to Bethlehem, witnessing their fatigue after finding no room in the inn and sharing their joy—and all of heaven's— at the birth of Jesus. Try to join the shepherds in praising God as they hear the angels singing and announcing the birth of our Savior, Messiah. Consider these responses and applications:

(a) Are you praising God for sending you a Savior?

_____

_____

_____

(b) Are you making a place for Jesus in your home and in your heart?

_____

_____

_____

(c) Are you receiving the peace that only Jesus can give you?

_____

_____

(d) Are you treasuring God's Word in your heart as Mary did?

_____

_____

_____

(e) Are you joyfully sharing with others that our Savior has COME?

_____

_____

_____

_____

_____

10. MY PERSONAL PRAYER RESPONSE. Talk to Jesus about your petitions and what actions you would like to take as a result of reflecting on the birth of your Savior. Then write your own prayer of thanksgiving in the space below.

_____

_____

_____

_____

_____

_____

_____

_____

PRAYER EXAMPLE

Dear Lord Jesus,

Thank you for coming to earth as a humble Baby and for all that you have taught me through your glorious birth in a stable.

Thank you for being the fulfillment of God's plan through all the ages.

Thank you that you are my Savior who died for the world's sins and for my sins so that I may have a relationship with you for all eternity. Thank you that you are the Christ, the Messiah who will reign throughout all eternity.

Thank you that you are my Lord and have a plan for my life. I give you my life now. I declare today that you are my personal Savior, Messiah, and Lord.

Help me to receive your joy and peace every day.

Help me to know and understand more of your Word so that I may share it with others. Now I pray for (include your intentions...)

7

The Circumcision, Naming
&
Presentation of Jesus

Connection Question

Have you ever attended a special celebration after a child has been baptized?
Please describe the event.

The Presentation of Jesus in the Temple[81]
by James Tissot, 1836-1894
United States Public Domain

Chapter Seven – The Circumcision
Naming and Presentation of Jesus

Eight Days Have Passed

The precious Baby Jesus has been born and rested contently in His mother's arms. Now eight days have passed, and Mary and Joseph have enjoyed each moment of the dear little Christ Child—after all He is God incarnate in soft infant skin. We can only imagine how blessed those days must have been for the Holy Family.

But, we cannot remain long at the manger because Luke quickly moves us to the next major event in the life of Christ. In fact, the next three stops on our journey are very important events that no devout Jewish parent would ever miss. Luke makes sure that we won't forget them either. Journeying with Blessed Mary, Saint Joseph and Baby Jesus—we now find ourselves on the way to the Circumcision, the Official Naming and the Presentation of their Son, the Son of God.

1. LUKE 2: 21-24. Read Luke 2: 21- 24 and **circle** the three important ceremonies in the life of the Holy Family that every new Jewish parent would attend. Share your thoughts.

_____

_____

_____

_____

_____

_____

Chapter Seven Questions

Luke 2: 21-24

²¹ After eight days had passed, it was time to circumcise the child; and he was called Jesus, the name given by the angel before he was conceived in the womb. ²² When the time came for their purification according to the law of Moses, they brought him up to Jerusalem to present him to the Lord ²³ (as it is written in the law of the Lord, "Every firstborn male shall be designated as holy to the Lord"), ²⁴ and they offered a sacrifice according to what is stated in the law of the Lord, "a pair of turtledoves or two young pigeons." NRSVCE

2. _THE CIRCUMCISION._ According to Luke 2: 21 and Genesis 17: 9-14, describe (a) when and (b) why Joseph and Mary had Jesus circumcised?

_____
_____
_____
_____
_____
_____
_____
_____

Genesis 17: 9-14. God said to Abraham, "As for you, you shall keep my covenant, you and your offspring after you throughout their generations. ¹⁰ This is my covenant, which you shall keep, between me and you and your offspring after you: Every male among you shall be circumcised. ¹¹ You shall circumcise the flesh of your foreskins, and it shall be a sign of the covenant between me and you. ¹² Throughout your generations every male among you shall be circumcised when he is eight days old, including the slave born in your house and the one bought with your money from any foreigner who is not of your offspring. ¹³ Both the slave born in your house and the one bought with your money must be circumcised. So shall my covenant be in your flesh an everlasting covenant. ¹⁴Any uncircumcised male who is not circumcised in the flesh of his foreskin shall be cut off from his people; he has broken my covenant."

Circumcised, Redeemed, and Purified

At the time of Jesus' birth, the Old Testament Mosaic law required every firstborn Jewish male to be **circumcised** and **redeemed,** which meant he was consecrated and presented back to God. In addition, the mother was required to be **purified** at the end of forty days if it was a boy, or after eighty days if it was a girl.

3. _THE THREE CEREMONIES._ Read the following chart that summarizes the three ceremonies the Mosaic Law required for all firstborn Jewish Males. Which ceremony do you find most surprising? Why?

_____
_____
_____
_____
_____
_____
_____
_____
_____
_____
_____

Mosaic Law Requirements for the Birth of a Child

Event and Scripture	After Birth	Place	Purpose	Who	Action
Circumcision and Naming Luke 2: 21 Genesis 17: 10-14:	8 days	Home	To enter the nation of Israel/ ratify Abrahamic Covenant— child belongs to God	Male child	Foreskin cut away by trained "mohel"
Presentation-Redemption Numbers 3: 41-51; Exodus 13: 13	30 (+) days	Home or Temple	To consecrate to God and buy back from God (redeem)	Firstborn male	Five silver shekels were given to the family priest
Purification Luke 2:22 Leviticus 12: 2-8	40 days male 80 days female	Temple in Jerusalem	To make the mother ceremonially clean to worship in the temple	Mother of baby	A one-year old lamb was sacrificed as a burnt offering; a young pigeon for a sin offering (if poor, two turtledoves were used for both offerings)

Ceremony #1: Circumcision and Naming

The **circumcision** took place at home on the eighth day after the birth, even if it fell on a Sabbath. It was performed by a trained person called a "mohel." Mary, Joseph, and the community knew that an uncircumcised male would be excluded from the Abrahamic covenant, citizenship in Israel, and participation in the Passover Meal (Exodus 12: 48). Thus, it was very important that Jesus, through circumcision, would be incorporated into the community of Israel.

In Jewish culture, the **naming of the baby** took place at the same time as the circumcision. Mary and Joseph had no choice; they knew by divine appointment what the Child was to be called. And so "He was named Jesus" which means *the Lord saves.* This was the name God chose for His son and told to both Mary and Joseph via an angel (see Luke 1: 30-31 and Matthew 1: 20-21).

On January 3 each year, the Catholic Church commemorates the **Most Holy Name of Jesus**. The *Catechism of the Catholic Church* points out the importance of that name:

"The name of 'Jesus' contains all: God and man and the whole economy of creation and salvation. To pray "Jesus" is to invoke Him and to call Him within us. **His name is the only one that contains the presence it signifies**. Jesus is the Risen One, and whoever invokes the name of Jesus is welcoming the Son of God who loved him and who gave himself up for him."[82]

4. THE NAME OF JESUS. Using the following chart, read the Scriptures and record the **key words** in each passage associated with the precious **Name of Jesus.**

_____
_____
_____
_____
_____
_____
_____

Scripture	Key Words & the Name of Jesus
John 1:12. "But to those who did accept him he gave power to become children of God, to those who believe in **his name [Jesus]**. NABRE	Example: *Power to become children of God*
John 16:23. "On that day you will not question me about anything. Amen, amen, I say to you, whatever you ask the Father in **my name [Jesus]** he will give you." NABRE	
Acts 4: 10-12. "Then all of you and all the people of Israel should know that it was in the **name of Jesus Christ** the Nazorean whom you crucified, whom God raised from the dead; in **his name,** this man stands before you healed. He is 'the stone rejected by you, the builders, which has become the cornerstone. There is no salvation through anyone else, nor is there any other **name** under heaven given to the human race by which we are to be saved." NABRE	
Romans 10:9. "For, if you confess with your mouth that **Jesus is Lord** and believe in your heart that God raised him from the dead, you will be saved." NABRE	
1 Cor. 6:11. "That is what some of you used to be; but now you have had yourselves washed, you were sanctified, you were justified in the **name of the Lord Jesus Christ** and in the Spirit of our God." NABRE	
Phil. 2: 9-11. "Because of this, God greatly exalted him and bestowed on him the **name** that is above every name, that at the **name of Jesus** every knee should bend, of those in heaven and on earth and under the earth, and every tongue confess that Jesus Christ is Lord, to the glory of God the Father." NABRE	
1 John 2:12. "I am writing to you, children, because your sins have been forgiven for **his [Jesus] name's sake**." NABRE	
1 John 5:11-13. "And this is the testimony: God gave us eternal life, and this life is in his Son. Whoever possesses the Son has life; whoever does not possess the Son of God does not have life. I write these things to you so that you may know that you have eternal life, you who believe in the **name of the Son of God**." NABRE	

The Name Jesus Fits His Divine Purpose

When God chose the name of Jesus, He chose it to fit His divine purpose and plan—the name means "God Saves."[83] This precious name of our Savior means more than we could ever imagine. The name of Jesus is associated with **power, prayer, healing, salvation, justification, exultation, forgiveness of sins** and **eternal life**. Fr. Francis Fernandez summarized all that is in the name of Jesus:

"After the circumcision of Jesus, his parents, Mary and Joseph, would say the name of Jesus for the first time, full of great devotion and love. And this is what we too must often do. To invoke his name is to be saved. To believe in this name is to be counted among the children of God. To pray in the name of Jesus is to be sure of being heard.

'Truly, truly, I say to you, if you ask anything of the Father, he will give it to you in my name.' In the name of Jesus, we obtain pardon for our sins and our souls are purified and made whole. The preaching of this name constitutes the whole essence of apostolate, 'for he is the goal of human history, the focal point of the desires of history and civilization, the centre of mankind, the joy of all hearts, and the fulfillment of all aspirations.' [84] Mankind finds in Jesus what it most needs and thirsts for: salvation, peace, happiness, the forgiveness of sins, freedom, understanding and friendship." [85]

St. Bernard left us with this sweet prayer to Jesus whose "Name is above every name" and at whose name "every knee should bend" (Philippians 2:10). What a wonderful prayer for adoration! [86]

"O Jesus,
How consoling you are to those who invoke you!
How good you are to those who seek you!
What will you not be to those who find you!
Only he who has felt it can know what it is
To languish in love for thee, O Jesus!"

5. *JERUSALEM.* (a) According to Luke 2: 22, why did Mary and Joseph go to Jerusalem? (b) Circle every time "the law" is mentioned in Luke 2: 22-24. What does the consistent mention of "the law" tell you about Jesus and His Holy family? (c) Knowing that the Holy Parents observed all of the religious ceremonies, what does this tell you about them?

_____

_____

_____

_____

_____

_____

Luke 2: 22-24. When the time came for their purification according to the law of Moses, they brought him up to Jerusalem to present him to the Lord [23] (as it is written in the law of the Lord, "Every firstborn male shall be designated as holy to the Lord"), [24] and they offered a sacrifice according to what is stated in the law of the Lord, "a pair of turtledoves or two young pigeons." NRSVCE

Jesus Came to Fulfil All the Law

According to Matthew 5: 17, Jesus said that He came "to fulfill the law" and fulfilling the law started at his birth. We can catch a better glimpse of His first coming to earth when we understand the Jewish culture in which Jesus was born. It also helps to recognize how Joseph and Mary followed the Mosaic Law, including the circumcision and naming of Baby Jesus, His presentation in the temple and Mary's purification.

5. _JERUSALEM._ (a) According to Luke 2: 22, why did Mary and Joseph go to Jerusalem? (b) Circle every time "the law" is mentioned in Luke 2: 22-24. What does the consistent mention of "the law" tell you about Jesus and His Holy family? (c) Knowing that the Holy Parents observed all of the religious ceremonies, what does this tell you about them?

_____

_____

_____

_____

_____

_____

Exodus 13: 1-2 and 12. The Lord said to Moses: 2Consecrate to me all the firstborn; whatever is the first to open the womb among the Israelites, of human beings and animals, is mine...12 you shall set apart to the Lord all that first opens the womb

Numbers 18: 15-16. The first issue of the womb of all creatures, human and animal, which is offered to the Lord, shall be yours; but the firstborn of human beings you shall redeem, and the firstborn of unclean animals you shall redeem. 16 Their redemption price, reckoned from one month of age, you shall fix at five shekels of silver, according to the shekel of the sanctuary (that is, twenty gerahs). NRSVCE

Note. Five shekels of silver was equal to 2 ounces of silver or about $34 today. The money was used to support the priests and the temple.

Ceremony #2: The Presentation or Redemption of Jesus

Luke doesn't mention the details of the "**redemption of the firstborn**" ceremony that we now call "**the Presentation**." When Joseph and Mary brought Jesus to the temple, they **presented** or consecrated Jesus to God, which meant they offered their child back to God who gave Him life, and they asked for God's blessing on Him. In addition, according to Mosaic Law, Mary and Joseph, like all parents of firstborn sons, would make an offering to God by paying a priestly family member the amount of five shekels (Numbers 18: 15-16). This meant they were **redeeming him or buying him back from God**. Isn't it amazing that almost 33 years later, it would be Jesus who would pay the price for our redemption by dying on the cross?

7. CEREMONY #3. According to Luke 2: 24, Mary came to the temple with a "pair of turtledoves." According to Leviticus 12: 2-8, (a) what was Mary's purpose in offering the turtledoves and (b) what does it says about her social status.

_____

_____

_____

_____

_____

_____

_____

_____

Leviticus 12: 2-8. The Lord spoke to Moses, saying: [2] Speak to the people of Israel, saying: If a woman conceives and bears a male child, she shall be ceremonially unclean seven days.... [3] On the eighth day the flesh of his foreskin shall be circumcised. [4] Her time of blood purification shall be thirty-three days; she shall not touch any holy thing, or come into the sanctuary, until the days of her purification are completed. [5] If she bears a female child, she shall be unclean two weeks, ... her time of blood purification shall be sixty-six days. [6]

When the days of her purification are completed, whether for a son or for a daughter, she shall bring to the priest at the entrance of the tent of meeting a lamb in its first year for a burnt offering, and a pigeon or a turtledove for a sin offering. [7] He shall offer it before the Lord, and make atonement on her behalf... This is the law for her who bears a child, male or female. [8] If she cannot afford a sheep, she shall take two turtledoves or two pigeons, one for a burnt offering and the other for a sin offering; and the priest shall make atonement on her behalf, and she shall be clean. NRSVCE

Ceremony #3: The Purification and Sin Offering

When God required a sin offering from a new mother, He did not mean that childbirth was wrong or somehow dirty. In the Jewish law, God made a clear distinction between sex and worship. Pagans often had sex orgies or engaged in prostitution and other immoral rites in their temples, as part of frenzied worship of fertility goddesses or other idols. God's laws forbid these immoral practices and require women to be pure. A woman was considered "ceremonially unclean" because of bodily secretions related to child birth. The law required a woman to be "clean" when she entered the temple for worship and to make a sin offering.

Leviticus 17: 11 reminds us that the heart and symbol of life is in the blood. In a representative way, a Jewish mother would offer her own life to God through the sacrificial blood offering of animals. The death of a pure and innocent animal would be offered as atonement for any sin and would fulfill the penalty of death required for atonement of sin. In the Old Testament law, God granted forgiveness to sinners who made the sin offering in faith. **In the New Testament, we learn that we no longer need the blood of animals as a sin offering. Instead, God sent Jesus to shed His blood as our sin offering** (See Hebrews 9: 11-14).

The Catholic Church celebrates the Presentation of Jesus and the Feast of the Purification of the Blessed Virgin Mary on February 2 of each year, when we read these same verses from Luke 2. This day is also called "Candlemas Day" because it is the time when candles used in the church are blessed and often includes a procession of candles. Most Reverend Fulton J. Sheen wrote of Mary, the Purification, and the Presentation:

"The mother who brought the 'Lamb of God' into the world had no lamb to offer—except the real Lamb of God. God was presented in the temple at the early age of 40 days. About 30 years later, He would claim the temple and use it as the symbol of His body, in which dwelt the fullness of Divinity."[87]

8. THE MAJESTIC NAME OF JESUS. Read Philippians 2: 5-11 and Palm 8: 1-9 and circle every mention and reference to the majestic name of Jesus, the Son of God, Sovereign Lord and the name that God chose for His Son.

_____

_____

_____

_____

_____

_____

_____

Philippians 2:5-11. Let the same mind be in you that was in Christ Jesus, 6 who, though he was in the form of God, did not regard equality with God as something to be exploited, 7 but emptied himself, taking the form of a slave, being born in human likeness. And being found in human form, 8 he humbled himself and became obedient to the point of death—even death on a cross. 9 Therefore God also highly exalted him and gave him the name that is above every name, 10 so that at the name of Jesus every knee should bend, in heaven and on earth and under the earth, 11 and every tongue should confess that Jesus Christ is Lord, to the glory of God the Father. NRSVCE

Psalm 8: 1-9. O Lord, our Sovereign, how majestic is your name in all the earth! You have set your glory above the heavens. 2 Out of the mouths of babes and infants you have founded a bulwark because of your foes, to silence the enemy and the avenger. 3 Then I look at your heavens, the work of your fingers, the moon and the stars that you have established; 4 what are human beings that you are mindful of them, mortals that you care for them? 5 Yet you have made them a little lower than God and crowned them with glory and honor. 6 You have given them dominion over the works of your hands; you have put all things under their feet, 7 all sheep and oxen, and also the beasts of the field, 8 the birds of the air, and the fish of the sea, whatever passes along the paths of the seas. 9 O Lord, our Sovereign, how majestic is your name in all the earth! NRSVCE

9. REFLECTION ON THE NAME OF JESUS. Try to imagine yourself joining Mary and Joseph with Baby Jesus at the three ceremonies. Picture Jesus being presented to God — the ONE who will later be presented to God for your sins. Consider the following applications:

(a) How glorious and meaningful is the name of Jesus to you?

_____

_____

_____

(b) Are you invoking the Holy Name of Jesus every day?

_____

_____

_____

(c) How can you speak His precious, majestic name more frequently?

_____

_____

_____

_____

10. PERSONAL PRAYER RESPONSE. Please write a prayer based on the glorious, majestic name of Jesus. See the following example.

_____

_____

_____

_____

_____

_____

_____

_____

_____

PRAYER EXAMPLE

Dear Jesus, my precious Lord, how I love you. How I love your name!
Your Name reminds me of Who you are.

Thank you that you are my SAVIOR—the one who pardons my sins.

Thank you for giving me the power and the right to become your child because I
believe in Your Name.

Thank you for the healing power in Your Name. Thank you that I have been
washed, sanctified and justified in your Holy Name.

Jesus, Your Name is above every name in heaven and on earth, and one day,
every knee shall bow to Your Name. Praise your Holy Name—the powerful and
precious name above all names.

As my Lord and Savior, I surrender my life to You. I believe that you died so I
might have forgiveness of sins. You are my Lord and Savior.

Please fulfill your plans for my life.

Now, I offer this prayer for the following intentions…

8

The Two Who Looked for His Coming

Connection Question

Have you ever yearned to see someone who lived far away?

The Presentation in the Temple[88]
by Philippe de Champaigne, 1648
United States Public Domain

Chapter Eight - Two Looked for His Coming

Still in the Temple

We remain in the temple for the presentation ceremony. It is a very special presentation—like none other. Mary and Joseph are presenting the Son of God back to the Father. At the same time, two very precious people recognize Baby Jesus as the Messiah. How did they know? Has someone told them? Let's join the Holy Family as we meet these two very special people, Simeon and Anna.

Chapter Eight Questions

1. LOOKING FOR THE LORD. Please read Luke 2: 25-40 and **circle** any references to the two who were awaiting the Lord's coming. (a) What are their names and (b) what do they have in common? (c) Share your thoughts.

_____
_____
_____
_____
_____
_____
_____
_____

Luke 2: 25-40

Now there was a man in Jerusalem whose name was Simeon; this man was righteous and devout, looking forward to the consolation of Israel, and the Holy Spirit rested on him. 26 It had been revealed to him by the Holy Spirit that he would not see death before he had seen the Lord's Messiah. 27Guided by the Spirit, Simeon came into the temple; and when the parents brought in the child Jesus, to do for him what was customary under the law, 28 Simeon took him in his arms and praised God, saying,

29"Master, now you are dismissing your servant in peace, according to your word; 30 for my eyes have seen your salvation, 31 which you have prepared in the presence of all peoples, 32 a light for revelation to the Gentiles and for glory to your people Israel." 33 And the child's father and mother were amazed at what was being said about him. 34 Then Simeon blessed them and said to his mother

Mary, "This child is destined for the falling and the rising of many in Israel, and to be a sign that will be opposed [35] so that the inner thoughts of many will be revealed—and a sword will pierce your own soul too."

[36] There was also a prophet, Anna the daughter of Phanuel, of the tribe of Asher. She was of a great age, having lived with her husband seven years after her marriage, [37] then as a widow to the age of eighty-four. She never left the temple but worshiped there with fasting and prayer night and day. [38] At that moment she came and began to praise God and to speak about the child to all who were looking for the redemption of Jerusalem.

[39] When they had finished everything required by the law of the Lord, they returned to Galilee, to their own town of Nazareth. [40] The child grew and became strong, filled with wisdom; and the favor of God was upon him. NRSVCE

> **Note.** "*Looking for the consolation of Israel*" (v. 25) refers to those devout Jews who were looking forward to the birth of the Messiah. They were expecting the Messiah who would restore God's rule to Israel.

2. SIMEON. Referring to Luke 2: 25-27, list at least 6 descriptors of Simeon in the chart below.

	Descriptors of Simeon (v. 25-27)
v. 25	1.
v. 25	2.
v. 25	3.
v. 25	4.
v. 26	5.
v. 27	6.

**3. JUST ANOTHER MOTHER.** (a) According to v. 27, who brought Simeon to the temple on that day and why? (b) <u>What prophetic insight</u> was revealed to Simeon? (c) W<u>ho </u>revealed it (v. 26)?

_____

_____

_____

_____

_____

_____

_____

Simeon

When the Holy Family entered the temple of Jerusalem, few even noticed their presence. Many people were standing at the porticoes listening to the Pharisees as they taught and discussed current religious issues and laws, while others traded in the Court of the Gentiles. Mary seemed like just another mother, among many, who came each day to be purified. Why would anyone even notice her or the little family?

Simeon noticed! The Holy Spirit had told him that he could expect to see the Messiah before he died. It was the Holy Spirit that led him to the temple that very day to witness something very special. When Simeon laid his eyes on the Christ Child, he knew the baby Jesus was the one he had longed for his entire life.

What do we know about Simeon? We know he was "righteous and devout" (v. 25) and probably rather old, according to his own words (v. 29). Most likely he was not a priest, but rather was a person who gave himself to prayer and doing pious works.[89] It was the extraordinary work of the Holy Spirit that moved on Simeon to pray in joy and then prophesy over this Baby—the Messiah.

4. *THE NUNC DIMITTIS.* (**a**) How would you describe the prayer recorded in
Luke 2: 29-32? (b) In the chart below, summarize the **major themes in each verse
of the Nunc Dimittis**.

_____

_____

_____

_____

_____

_____

_____

Luke 2:29-32. "Master, now you are dismissing your servant[a] in peace,
according to your word; [30] for my eyes have seen your salvation, [31] which you
have prepared in the presence of all peoples, [32] a light for revelation to the
Gentiles and for glory to your people Israel."

MAJOR THEMES IN THE NUNC DIMITTIS	
v. 29	**Theme 1:**
v. 30	**Theme 2:**
v. 31	**Theme 3:**
v. 32	**Theme 4:**
v. 32	**Theme 5:**

Simeon's Prayer – The Nunc Dimittis

Simeon's prayer from Luke 2: 29-32 is one of the great canticles—little songs or prayers of the Church. It is called the *Nunc Dimittis* because in the Latin translation of the Bible (v. 29), the first words are "Nunc Dimittis," which mean "now dismiss your servant." (In other words, Simeon was saying to the Lord, "Now I am ready to die; you can dismiss me Lord, I have seen the Savior.") This prayer is prayed every night by all priests, religious, and laity who pray the *Liturgy of the Hours,* also called *The Divine Office).* Each of the themes or phrases of the *Nunc Dimittis* prayer have great meaning.

5. READY TO GO IN PEACE. (a) Why is Simeon so thankful (v. 29-32) that he prays he is ready to die? ("go in peace")? (b) What role does Simeon say the Child will fulfill (v. 30)? (c) Who is the salvation intended to reach (v. 30-32)?

_____
_____
_____
_____
_____
_____
_____
_____

6. PROPHECIES FULFILLED. Read the prophecies below from Isaiah 42: 6 and 49: 6. List the same themes found in the Nunc Dimittis of Luke 2: 31-32.

_____
_____
_____
_____
_____
_____

Isaiah 42: 6. I am the Lord, I have called you in righteousness, I have taken you by the hand and kept you; I have given you as a covenant to the people, **a light to the nations** to open the eyes that are blind… NRSVCE

Isaiah 49: 6. The Lord says, "It is too light a thing that you should be my servant to raise up the tribes of Jacob and to restore the survivors of Israel; **I will give you as a light to the nations, that my salvation may reach to the end of the earth."** NRSVCE

The Nunc Dimittis Reflects Isaiah's Prophecies

Many people of Simeon's time would probably have forgotten the prophetic words recorded in Isaiah about the Messiah who would come "to the ends of the earth" and be a "revelation to the nations [Gentiles]." Certainly, the exclusive-thinking Pharisees would find Simeon's words scandalous since the Pharisees believed the Messiah was coming only for Israel. However, if they looked closely, they would see the words and themes of Simeon's prophecy had come directly from the great prophecies of Isaiah.

7. SIMEON'S MESSAGE TO MARY. How did Mary and Joseph respond to Simeon's words of prophecy (v. 33)?

_____
_____
_____
_____
_____
_____
_____
_____

Amazed

Although Mary and Joseph had great revelation from God through the angel's messages, they were still amazed at what Simeon said and how he knew such things. Did you ever have a situation in your life that was hard to understand at the time? Sometimes we get so involved in day-to-day living that when highly significant events happen, we can't understand the full meaning. Often it is for the best that we can't comprehend all future impact. In this case, Simeon's words for Mary were hard to comprehend at the time, but the day would come when the Blessed Mother could understand exactly what they meant.

8. FOUR PARTS. List the four parts of Simeon's prophecy to Mary in Luke 2: 34-35 and then star the words that would be hardest for Mary to comprehend.

Simeon's Four-Part Prophecy to Mary – Luke 2: 34-35

v. 34

_____

_____

v. 34

_____

_____

v. 35

_____

_____

v. 35

_____

_____

Luke 2: 34-35. Then Simeon blessed them and said to his mother Mary, "This child is destined for the falling and the rising of many in Israel, and to be a sign that will be opposed [35] so that the inner thoughts of many will be revealed — and a sword will pierce your own soul too."

A Sign to Be Opposed

In Luke 2: 34-35, Simeon prophesied that Jesus would be **"a sign that will be opposed,"** meaning that even though He came to bring salvation to all, there would be division, and many would not receive Him. Simeon also said, "this child is destined for the falling and rising of many." **The rising** of many (see Malachi 4:2) refers to those who would accept Jesus in faith to set them free from sin in this life and raise them up to eternal life. **The fall of many** (see Isaiah 8:14-15) refers to those who would stubbornly reject Jesus leading to eternal death.[90]

To Mary, Simeon said, **"a sword will pierce your own soul,"** foretelling the unspeakable pain she would share in her son's sufferings. But her pain would happen with purpose so that **"the thoughts of many hearts will be revealed."** Thus, the attitude toward Jesus would show whether one receives Him or rejects Him and ultimately receives or rejects all of God's revelation.

Jesus as an adult would fulfill Simeon's prophecy. In his own words of John 3: 17-21, Jesus said: "Indeed, God did not send the Son into the world to condemn the world, but in order that the world might be saved through him. [18] Those who believe in him are not condemned; but those who do not believe are condemned already, because they have not believed in the name of the only Son of God."

The Prayerful Recognize the Lord

Although Bethlehem would have no home for Jesus for a time, not all the people of Jerusalem would be opposed to Jesus. Many would accept Him and live for Him. Thus, Simeon reminds us today that there are many single-minded and prayerful hearts in our world, who are awaiting the Lord and it is "the prayerful nature of Simeon, which most easily recognizes Our Lord" in the normal aspects of daily living.[91]

Today and every day, and especially during Advent, we can pray this canticle.

The Nunc Dimittis

Lord, now let your servant go in peace.
Your word has been fulfilled.
My own eyes have seen the salvation
Which you have prepared in the sight of every people:
A light to reveal you to the nations
And the glory of your people Israel.

Glory to the Father, and to the Son, and to the Holy Spirit,
As it was in the beginning, is now, and will be forever. Amen.

Anna

Luke, who likes to share twin episodes takes us next to meet another person who has been prayerfully awaiting the Messiah her entire life. She is praying in the Temple.

9. ANNA. Reread Luke 2: 36-38 below and underline all the facts about Anna. Then list below at least seven facts about Anna from v. 36-37.

FACTS ABOUT ANNA - LUKE 2: 36-37	
v. 36	
v. 36	
v. 36	
v. 36	
v. 37	
v. 37	
v. 37	

Luke 2: 36-40. [36] There was also a prophet, Anna the daughter of Phanuel, of the tribe of Asher. She was of a great age, having lived with her husband seven years after her marriage, [37] then as a widow to the age of eighty-four. She never left the temple but worshiped there with fasting and prayer night and day. [38] At that moment she came and began to praise God and to speak about the child to all who were looking for the redemption of Jerusalem. [39] When they had finished everything required by the law of the Lord, they returned to Galilee, to their own town of Nazareth. [40] The child grew and became strong, filled with wisdom; and the favor of God was upon him. NRSVCE

Note. Anna was from the Tribe of _Asher_ (Luke 2: 36). Asher was a highly esteemed tribe of Israel who were assigned the role of providing food for the kings (Genesis 49: 20). This would mean that Anna had been part of a much-respected family, who served God. Her father's name "Phanuel" in Hebrew means "the face of God" so he was likely a man who loved to worship and behold the face of God. So Anna wanted to stay in the temple and worship in the presence of God.

10. IN THE TEMPLE. (a) Since Anna "never left the temple," what two things did she do on a daily basis? (b) What does Anna's life tell you about her relationship with God (v. 37)? (c) How does Anna respond to seeing Baby Jesus (v. 38)?

_____

_____

_____

_____

_____

_____

Worshipper and Prophetess

Anna was a woman who persevered in worship and service to God. She seemed like a very ordinary person, but NOT to God. God revealed His plan and His Son to her long before others would find out about the birth of the Messiah. Anna was called a prophetess or one who prophesies. To prophesy means to speak forth or declare God's message, will or purpose.[92]

There are only nine prophetesses named in Scripture: **Miriam**, sister of Moses and Aaron (Exodus 15:20), **Deborah**, a judge of Israel, (Judges 4:4), **Huldah**, the wife of the King's right-hand man (2 Kings 22:14), **Isaiah's wife** (Isaiah 8:1-3), **Anna** (Luke 2:36), and **Philip's four unmarried daughters** (Acts 21: 8-9). Rabbinical literature also lists Sarah, (wife of Abraham), Hannah (mother of Samuel), Esther, and Abigail (one of David's wives) as prophetesses, but they are not called such in Scripture.

Anna's spiritual insight came out of the time she spent communing with God in worship, fasting and intercession. According to Most Rev. Alban Goodier, S. J., Anna's faithfulness in worship and service to God represents the many women in the Church who are and have always been a great source of blessing—women who live their faith by their prayers and by their active cooperation with God. Thus, they are a true support of the church. [93]

Both Anna and Simeon stand out as role models of senior citizens whose prayer and faith-lives are very deep and who are used mightily by God. Although our culture emphasizes youthfulness, this was not true at the time of Jesus. Older ones were valued for their wisdom, practical advice and life-time contributions. God calls us to value the insight of the older individuals in our lives. They are treasures of support and advice and often have Godly words or insights for those who take the time to listen to their wisdom.

11. _REFLECTION ON WAITING._ (a) What do Simeon and Anna teach about waiting for the Lord? (b) When you know that at the end of life you will meet the Lord and give an account of what you have done, what difference does that make in how you live each day? (c) Read Titus 2: 11-15 and 2 Timothy 4: 7-9 and circle all the ways you can wait for Christ's Second Coming.

_____

_____

_____

_____

_____

_____

_____

_____

_____

_____

_____

Titus 2: 11-15. For the grace of God has appeared, bringing salvation to all, 12training us to renounce impiety and worldly passions, and in the present age to live lives that are self-controlled, upright, and godly, 13 while we wait for the blessed hope and the manifestation of the glory of our great God and Savior, Jesus Christ. 14 He it is who gave himself for us that he might redeem us from all iniquity and purify for himself a people of his own who are zealous for good deeds. 15 Declare these things; exhort and reprove with all authority. Let no one look down on you. NRSVCE

2 Timothy 4: 7-9. I have fought the good fight, I have finished the race, I have kept the faith. 8 From now on there is reserved for me the crown of righteousness, which the Lord, the righteous judge, will give me on that day, and not only to me but also to all who have longed for his appearing. NRSVCE

Like Simeon and Anna, We Await His Second Coming

"Christ has died, Christ has risen, Christ will come again" are the words we say in Mass as a responsorial after the consecration. "Christ will come again in glory to judge the living and the dead and His Kingdom will have no end" are the words we say in the Creed to reaffirm our belief that Christ will come again. In a similar way as Simeon and Anna, we look forward to Christ's coming. When Jesus came the first time, He came as a lamb in humility and lowliness. When He comes a second time, He will come in glory as the King of Kings and the Lord of Lords. As the Catechism explains, He will "reveal the secret dispositions of hearts" and "in the presence of Christ, who is Truth itself, the truth of each man's relationship with God will be laid bare."[94] We should have a desire for His return as we will be united with Him in Glory forever and His justice will triumph.

Jesus' Return in Glory is called both the "Day of Salvation" for those who live for Him and follow Him (Revelation 21:1) and the "Day of Judgment" for those who refuse to receive the Good News (2 Thessalonians 1: 6-10). On that Day when he comes again, Jesus will give us an imperishable inheritance (1 Peter 1: 3-4), permanent citizenship in Heaven, and new bodies (Philippians 3: 20-21, 1 Corinthians 15: 51-55). We will live happily in His presence forever (Revelation 21: 3-4).

12. _MY PERSONAL PRAYER RESPONSE._ Please write a prayer from you heart on how you are waiting for the Lord. See the following example.

_____

_____

_____

_____

_____

_____

_____

_____

_____

_____

PRAYER EXAMPLE

Dear Jesus, my precious and glorious Lord, I love you.

I long for your Second Coming and the full establishment of Your Kingdom.

Help me to live in your love, to stand strong, to have mercy on those who waiver, to help others, and to abhor all evil.

Keep me from stumbling. I want my life to be unblemished in your presence. I look to you for joy.

From my heart, I pray the words of this hymn to you.

WHEN MARY BROUGHT HER TREASURE [95]

Stanza 1

When Mary brought her treasure
Unto the holy place,
No eye of man could measure
The joy upon her face.
He was but six weeks old,
Her plaything and her pleasure,
Her silver and her gold.

Stanza 2

Then Simeon, on him gazing
With wonder and with love,
His aged voice up-raising
Gave thanks to God above:
"Now welcome sweet release!
For I, my Savior praising,
May die at last in peace."

Stanza 3

As by the sun in splendor
The flags of night are furled.
So darkness shall surrender
To Christ who lights the world,
To Christ the star of day,
Who once was small and tender,
A candle's gentle ray.

9

Magi Pay Homage, Herod Kills to Keep Homage

Connection Question

How long have you been singing "We Three Kings of Orient"?

Note: We Three Kings of Orient was written in 1887 by Rev. John Henry Hopkins, Jr., Episcopalian bishop and author of many hymns and canticles.

Journey of the Magi [96]
by James Tissot, 1836-1902
United States Public Domain

Chapter Nine –Magi Pay Homage
Herod Kills to Keep Homage

The Feast of the Epiphany

The next event on our Advent journey is the coming of the Magi, also called Wise Men, who "traveled afar" to see the new born king. We must turn to Matthew to catch a glimpse of the event, because Luke is silent about their visit.

The Church celebrates the coming of the Magi on the Feast of the Epiphany. In New Testament Greek, the word Epiphany means "manifestation." Thus, according to the Catechism of the Catholic Church, when we celebrate Epiphany, we celebrate the manifestation or revelation of Jesus Christ "as the Messiah of Israel, the Son of God and the Savior of the world.".[97]

The Magi were the first fruits of the Gentiles who came to worship the newly born Savior and King. They represent the nations and peoples who are sitting in the darkness of mythologies, vain philosophies, idolatries, immoralities and demonic captivities of all kinds. These are the ones that Jesus came to show the light and save them from their sins. They need the Light in their great darkness as prophesied in Isaiah 9:2 and repeated in Matthew 4: 16. "[T]he people who sat in darkness have seen a great light, and for those who sat in the region and shadow of death light has dawned." The manifestation of Jesus as the Savior and Messiah and Light in great darkness is the meaning of Epiphany. Today, more than ever, we need Jesus as Savior, Messiah and Light in our great cultural darkness

Chapter Nine Questions

1. THE WISE MEN (MAGI) COME TO WORSHIP. Read Matthew 2: 1-15 and (a) circle what you find most interesting. (b) When did the wise men come (v. 1)? (c) Where was their home (v. 1)? (d) What brought them to Jerusalem (v. 2)?

_____

_____

_____

_____

_____

_____

Matthew 2: 1-15

In the time of King Herod, after Jesus was born in Bethlehem of Judea, wise men from the East came to Jerusalem, 2 asking, "Where is the child who has been born king of the Jews? For we observed his star at its rising and have come to pay him homage." 3When King Herod heard this, he was frightened, and all Jerusalem with him; 4 and calling together all the chief priests and scribes of the people, he inquired of them where the Messiah was to be born. 5 They told him, "In Bethlehem of Judea; for so it has been written by the prophet: 6'And you, Bethlehem, in the land of Judah, are by no means least among the rulers of Judah; for from you shall come a ruler who is to shepherd my people Israel.'" NRSVCE

7 Then Herod secretly called for the wise men and learned from them the exact time when the star had appeared. 8 Then he sent them to Bethlehem, saying, "Go and search diligently for the child; and when you have found him, bring me word so that I may also go and pay him homage." 9 When they had heard the king, they set out; and there, ahead of them, went the star that they had seen at its rising, until it stopped over the place where the child was. 10 When they saw that the star had stopped, they were overwhelmed with joy. 11On entering the house, they saw the child with Mary his mother; and they knelt down and paid him homage. Then, opening their treasure chests, they offered him gifts of gold, frankincense, and myrrh. 12 And having been warned in a dream not to return to Herod, they left for their own country by another road.

13 Now after they had left, an angel of the Lord appeared to Joseph in a dream and said, "Get up, take the child and his mother, and flee to Egypt, and remain there until I tell you; for Herod is about to search for the child, to destroy him." 14 Then Joseph got up, took the child and his mother by night, and went to Egypt, 15 and remained there until the death of Herod. This was to fulfill what had been spoken by the Lord through the prophet, "Out of Egypt I have called my son."

2. THE VISIT. (a) What did the wise men ask the people of Jerusalem (v. 2) **(b)** What reason did the wise men give for their visit (v. 2)? **(c)** Who was troubled and why were they troubled (v. 3)? **(d)** How did Herod respond to the wise men's visit and questions (v. 4)?

_____
_____
_____
_____
_____

Information on the Wise Men (Magi)

The wise men came to Jerusalem "in the days of King Herod," which indicates Herod the Great was the ruler of the area at the time of their coming. Herod was declared King of Judea by the Roman Senate in 40 BC and reigned in Jerusalem from 37 BC until after Christ's birth, around 4 BC. Herod was an evil, ruthless king, who was responsible for killing all the male infants (called the Holy Innocents) in an attempt to kill Jesus.

The *wise men* are also called the *Magi* in many Bible translations. ("Magoi" is the word used in New Testament Greek.) Both names are the traditional terms given to those who came from the East. These wise men were astronomers, who while studying the movement of planets and stars, came upon a magnificent star. Many, including Church Father Clement of Alexandria believe they were from **Persia**, near China (hence we sing, "We three kings of Orient are...").[98] They may have traveled hundreds of miles. Others believe they came from **Babylon** because of the Babylonian interest in astronomy. They could have learned of the Messianic prophecies from the Jews who were left behind during the Babylonian captivity. St. Justin Martyr suggests they may have come a shorter distance, possibly from the **Arabian Peninsula** because the gifts they brought were associated with camel caravans coming from Median in northwest Arabia or Sheba in southwest Arabia as Isaiah 60: 1-6 points out:

> **Isaiah 60: 1-6.** Arise, shine; for your light has come, and the glory of the Lord has risen upon you. 2 For darkness shall cover the earth, and thick darkness the peoples; but the Lord will arise upon you, and his glory will appear over you. 3 Nations shall come to your light, and kings to the brightness of your dawn... 6 A multitude of camels shall cover you, the young camels of Midian and Ephah; all those from Sheba shall come. They shall bring gold and frankincense and shall proclaim the praise of the Lord.

Both the people and Herod were troubled because they did not know about the great happening of the Messiah's birth before the Magi came. Herod was even more troubled because he was the king and wanted to remain king. He may have heard of the Old Testament prophecies about a star, the rise of a new ruler, and the disaster for his family (Numbers 24:17-19). The people of Jerusalem may have been troubled because they knew Herod was capable of killing anyone who might try to compete with him.

3. **_THE STAR._** Read Matthew 2: 5-6, Numbers 24:17, and Micah 5: 1 and explain (a) why you think the Magi knew the star represented the Messiah and (b) why were the wise men so wise.

_____

_____

_____

_____

_____

_____

Matthew 2: 5-6. They said to him, "In Bethlehem of Judea, for thus it has been written through the prophet: 6 'And you, Bethlehem, land of Judah, are by no means least among the rulers of Judah; since from you shall come a ruler, who is to shepherd my people Israel.'"

Numbers 24:17. A star shall come out of Jacob, and a scepter shall rise out of Israel.

Micah 5:1. But you, O Bethlehem of Ephrathah, who are one of the little clans of Judah, from you shall come forth for me one who is to rule in Israel, whose origin is from of old, from ancient days.

Note. Ephrathah (Micah 5:1) is the district where Bethlehem is located. This Micah prophecy is very specific. Today, it would be like specifying a small suburb in a large city. As the prophecy indicated, though the size of the city was small, the ruler to arise there would be great. The distance traveled could have been about 120 miles.

New Information Confirms St. Justin Martyr's Assertion

The book *Mystery of the Magi: The Quest to Identify the Three Wise Men* by Fr. Dwight Longenecker (2017) adds some additional historical information to their mystery. His extensive research suggests the Magi likely came from a Middle Eastern kingdom called Nabataea, which at the time spread across northern Arabia to Syria.[99] (This was the area St. Justin Martyr suggested was their homeland.)

A large number of Jewish immigrants had lived in Nabataea after escaping the Babylonian captivity, as did many other Persians, Greeks and Babylonians—thus, forming a cultural and religious melting pot. At the time of Jesus, the Nabataean kingdom was a neighbor to Israel. Herod's son Antipas had married a Nabatean princess, the daughter of Nabatean King Aretas IV. Thus, Aretas IV and his advisors (i.e., wise men or scholars in history, astronomy/astrology, religion, science, etc.) would naturally have an interest in everything happening in Judea. They would have known of prophecies about a great king arising among the Jews.[100] When the wise men saw a super star or supernova (e.g., from a conjunction of planets Jupiter and Saturn) or other bright star (e.g., possibly even an angel), it signalled a momentous event—which they surmised was the birth of a Jewish baby who would be king. So, when they told King Aretas IV, he may have sent his Magi on a diplomatic mission with a huge crowd of servants and gifts to Herod as they likely believed the newborn was Herod's son. With that type of entourage appearing in the city, the entire population would have been interested and alarmed.

4. THE NUMBERS. (a) Based on Matthew 2: 1-15, how many wise men do you think came to Jerusalem and (b) why.

_____
_____
_____
_____
_____
_____

Three or More?

How many magi were there? Some early paintings of the second century show four[101] while some medieval Eastern lists mention twelve.[102] However, an exact number was never specified in the Gospels. The Nabatean connection suggests an entourage. Three has been mentioned most frequently because of the three different gifts.[103] Even though names were never specified for the magi, tradition since the sixth century has assigned them names: *Casper*, the young beardless one bringing frankincense, *Balthasar*, the middle-aged one carrying Myrrh, and *Melchior*, the eldest bearded one porting gold.[104]

The Catholic Church commemorates the coming of the magi on January 6, but in the United States, Epiphany is celebrated on the Sunday nearest January 6. The exact date of the magi's arrival is not as important as the message. Matthew stresses the significance of their coming by showing them as the first gentiles to adore our Savior. St. Augustine said that the magi were the "first fruits of the Gentiles," and the first of many who Jesus said would come "from the East and West" to "eat with Abraham and Isaac and Jacob in the kingdom of heaven."[105] The *Catechism of the Catholic Church* emphasizes they were the ones seeking the King of all nations:

"In the magi, representatives of the neighboring pagan religions, the Gospel sees the first-fruits of the nations, who welcome the good news of salvation through the Incarnation. The magi's coming to Jerusalem in order to pay homage to the king of the Jews shows that they seek in Israel, in the messianic light of the star of David, the one who will be the king of the nations."[106]

<u>5. *HEROD.*</u> (a) Describe the beginning of Herod's deceitfulness in v. 7-8. (b)Why do you think Herod did not accompany the magi in search of the Christ Child? (c) How did the magi know not to go back to Herod?

_____

_____

_____

_____

_____

_____

_____

The Wise Men, Chief Priests & Scribes Knew the Scriptures

The chief priests and scribes were the Jewish aristocracy and theological scholars. Herod called them because he knew they would know about the prophecies. These included Micah 5: 2, as well as the many other Scriptures that pointed out the Messiah would come through David's lineage to Bethlehem. **The magi were paraphrasing Scripture** in Matthew 2: 5-6 and probably had studied ancient Jewish manuscripts, as well as other manuscripts from religions of the world. They likely learned about the Scriptures and the coming of the Messiah from the Jews who had escaped the Babylonian captivity.

6. THE MAGI FIND JESUS. (a) How did the wise men know where to find Jesus and where did they find Him (v. 9)? (b) How did they respond (v. 10-11)? (c) Where did they go when they left Jesus, and why (v. 12)? (d) Do you think the bright star was the light of an angel, an astrological event or other phenomena? (Any could have been sent from God.) Explain your answer.

_____

_____

_____

_____

_____

When?

Scripture provides only limited information about the magi. You may be surprised to learn that they may not have come at the exact night of Christ's birth, although we include them in our Nativity scenes. Some scholars believe that the star appeared many months before Christ's birth and then guided the magi to the manger shortly after Jesus was born. St. Augustine suggests the magi came—after the circumcision, or even on the thirteenth day after the Nativity—the day the Church celebrates their coming.[107] Still others believe the magi appeared in Bethlehem at least 40 days after the birth, which allowed time for the presentation of Jesus in the temple and Mary's purification and recovery from the birth (then she could travel easily).[108]

Evidence in Matthew 2: 11 indicates that Mary and Joseph may have been staying at a home by the time the wise men arrived. In Luke 2: 24, Mary had only the two turtle doves to offer at her purification instead of a lamb— if the wise man had come already, they could have purchased a lamb with the gifts of gold. In Matthew 2: 16 the magi's inquiries (and possibly large entourage) frightened Herod and the entire town. Their statements inflamed Herod's desire to get rid of any new-born Messiah. Thus, Herod ordered the killing of all boys "in and around Bethlehem who were two years old and under, according to the time he had learned from the wise men" (Matthew 2: 16).

7. THE GIFTS. See below for the gifts presented to Jesus (v. 11) and the symbolism for each. Please add the meaning of each gift related to Jesus' purpose in coming.

Symbolism of the Gifts	Scripture Reference	Meaning Related to Jesus' Purpose
Gold - The finest gift for a <u>KING.</u>	**Psalm 72: 15.** "...The King...Long may he live, may **gold** from Arabia be given to him, may prayer be made for him continually, and may blessings be evoked for him all day long."	
Frankincense - A gift of worship for a <u>DEITY</u>.	**Isaiah 60: 6.** "a multitude of camels will cover you...all from Sheba shall come. They shall bring gold and **frankincense** and shall proclaim the praise of the LORD."	
Myrrh - An expensive gift and strongly fragranced spice used to prepare bodies for <u>BURIAL.</u>	**John 19: 39-40.** "Nicodemus, who had at first come to Jesus by night, also came, bringing a mixture of myrrh and aloes, weighing about a hundred pounds. They took the body of Jesus and wrapped it with the spices in linen cloths, according to the burial custom of the Jews." NRSVCE	

Gifts for an Eternal King: True God and True Man

The gifts offered to Jesus are deeply significant. They symbolized that Jesus was God, the King, and a man who came to die. In Israel at the time of Jesus' birth, incense was offered only to God — incense offered in any other way was an abomination to Jehovah. Thus, the offering of **frankincense** signified that the magi were expressing worship to God.[109] **Gold** was the offering given to Kings. By offering gold, the magi were acknowledging that Jesus was born to be the King. Finally, by offering **myrrh**, a spice and perfume used for embalming, the magi were venerating the human nature of Jesus and declaring in advance His passion and death. In addition, Myrrh was used to anoint the alter of the Tabernacle and the priests (Exodus 30: 23-33). Therefore, the magi offered gold to the king, incense to God, and myrrh to the man destined to die.[110]

According to St. Gregory the Great, the three gifts can also symbolize the gifts we present to Christ.[111] [112] Gold for King Jesus — we offer him to be the king and ruler of our lives and our speech every day. Frankincense for Lord Jesus — we offer Him our adoration and devotion about all else in our lives and our prayers. Myrrh for Jesus, our Savior, who died for our sins and saves us for all eternity — we offer Him our lives, accept his forgiveness and acknowledge that without Him, our lives have no meaning. Since, "Jesus Christ is the same yesterday and today and forever…Through him, then, let us continually offer a sacrifice of praise to God, that is, the fruit of lips that confess his name (Hebrews 8, 13: 15).

Note: The Gifts. Fr. Longenecker points out that the three gifts—**gold, frankincense and myrrh** were the finest exports of the Nabatean Kingdom at the time.[113] The Nabateans controlled the gold-rich areas of northern Arabia and the flow of gold in the trade routes from East Africa. Nabatean **gold** was the purest of all! Thus, gold would represent the very best that King Aretas IV could offer a newborn king. In addition, **frankincense** was used for burning incense in ceremonies of many religions and **myrrh** was used as a medical treatment for pain, wounds and infections. Both were grown and harvested only once per year in Nabataea. They were very valuable commodities and would be a precious gift to a newborn king from the Nabataean king and his magi.

---

8. INTO EGYPT. (a) When and why did Joseph take Mary and Jesus to Egypt (v. 13-14)? (b) What does v. 13 reveal about Joseph's leadership and faithfulness to God? (c) How long did the Holy Family stay in Egypt (v. 15)?

_____

_____

_____

_____

_____

Unbelievers Try to Silence the Truth, Christians Follow God

In Matthew 2: 15, it is clear that Jesus fulfilled Biblical prophecy and followed in Biblical tradition. Jesus relived the Exodus experience of Moses and Israel by being "called out of Egypt." Thus, Matthew was highlighting that Jesus was greater than Moses and fulfilled Israel's *sonship* relationship with God.[114] Like Moses, Jesus had been saved as a child from a king's murderous plot (Exodus 1), fled to Egypt to find refuge (Exodus 2), and was appointed by God to proclaim the New Covenant Law (Exodus 20), meaning. Jesus was the expected Messiah.

Like many people do today, Herod tried to silence the truth of God. His own pride and desire for power kept him from coming to the One who has the power of the universe for all eternity—Jesus, the King of Kings and Lord of Lords. As Christians, we choose to follow the King of the Universe. However, like the Magi and the Holy Family, we often have to change our plans to follow God. According to St. John Chrysostom, we should not be surprised by this, but rather should be on the lookout for dangers, oppositions and temptations.[115]

Mary and Joseph knew that Jesus was the Messiah. Yet even they had to follow God's plan and endure much inconvenience and hardship. Taking a baby over hills and rough terrains in the middle of the night was no easy task. Leaving family and friends at such a young age probably gave them many anxious feelings. However, Mary and Joseph constantly made decisions to follow God's guidance, even when it wasn't convenient or easy for them. They simply trusted God to lead them step-by-step along the way, as we must do.

9. MASSACRE OF THE HOLY INNOCENTS. (a) According to Matthew 2: 16-18, how did Herod respond when the wise men did not return to him. (v. 16) (b) How was the Jeremiah 31:15 prophecy fulfilled in the massacre of the children?

_____
_____
_____
_____
_____
_____
_____

Matthew 2: 16-18. When Herod saw that he had been tricked by the wise men, he was infuriated, and he sent and killed all the children in and around Bethlehem who were two years old or under, according to the time that he had learned from the wise men. 17 Then was fulfilled what had been spoken through the prophet Jeremiah: 18 "A voice was heard in Ramah, wailing and loud lamentation, Rachel weeping for her children; she refused to be consoled, because they are no more."

Jeremiah 31:15. Thus says the Lord: A voice is heard in Ramah, lamentation and bitter weeping. Rachel is weeping for her children; she refuses to be comforted for her children, because they are no more.

> Note: *Rachel* **was the wife of Jacob.** He was later called Israel and became the father of the 12 tribes of Israel. *Ramah* was called "a city of sorrow" as it was the place of an Assyrian attack (8 BC) and the place where the Babylonians bound and took captives. Therefore, in the prophecy, Rachel represents all the mothers of Israel weeping for their children. The village of Ramah is 5 miles north of Jerusalem and is the place where Rachel was buried. (Later, Rachel's tomb was moved to the Bethlehem area, where it was when Matthew was writing.) Thus, Biblical prophecy was fulfilled in Matthew 2:17 as written over 700 years earlier in Jeremiah 31:15.

The Feast of the Holy Innocents

The Feast of the Holy Innocents is also called the Feast of the Holy Children by the Eastern Church. It is celebrated on December 28th each year to commemorate the lives and deaths of these murdered children. They were truly martyrs as they died for Jesus Christ and in His place.

10. TO CHRIST. In the space below, summarize the response of the following people to Jesus, the Christ Child.

The People	Their Response to Christ based on Matthew 2: 1-18
(a) Herod (v. 16-18):	
(b) Chief Priest and Scribes (v. 4-6):	
(c) All of Jerusalem (v. 3):	
(d) The Wise Men (v. 11)	

Reactions to Jesus: Hatred, Indifference or Worship

Herod was always suspicious of anyone who might undermine his power and so he often eliminated them. He **hated** the possibility of a Messiah. The crimes of Herod were so horrific that ordering the death of babies was insignificant to him. Since Jerusalem was a small city, scholars estimated that 20 to 25 babies were killed at Herod's command. [116]

Herod murdered his wife Marianne and his mother-in-law Alexandra; he arranged the assassinations of his sons Antipater, Alexander, and Aristobulus.[117] With a play on words, Roman Emperor Augustus quipped, "It was safer to be a hog (*hus* in Latin) of Herod's than to be his son (*huios* in Latin)."[118]

The religious rulers were **indifferent** to Jesus. They spent their time discussing or debating legal issues and rituals. Jesus meant nothing to them in their daily existence.[119] The people were frightened or troubled of something new. They likely thought, "change is never good."

The wise men came to **worship**. They traveled a good distance on camels and then bowed down before Jesus offering the choicest gifts to Him in their adoration.

11. REFLECTION AND MY RESPONSE TO JESUS. Now is a good time to consider how you respond to Jesus? Pray with any of the words below.

(a) *Jesus, I want to follow you and love you, not live for myself like Herod did.*

_____

(b) *Jesus, be the King and joy of my life. I do not want to even look like the religious rulers who were only interested in their own lives and arguments*

_____

(c) *Jesus, You are my Lord. Like the wise men did, I will adore and worship you. I will give you all the best of me.*

_____

(d) *Jesus my Savior, I am willing to accept your plans for my life. Like the Holy Family and the Magi, I am willing to go a new direction when you lead me.*

_____

_____

12. _MY PERSONAL PRAYER RESPONSE._ Please write a prayer to Jesus expressing your desire to adore, worship, serve and joyfully accept His plans for your life. See the following example.

_____
_____
_____
_____
_____
_____
_____
_____
_____
_____

PRAYER EXAMPLE

Dear Jesus, I praise you.
You are the Messiah, the hope of all mankind, the ONE who will reign throughout eternity. You came to die for my sins that I might live forever. I want to worship you more this year. You are my SAVIOR.

I give my life to you. I am willing to be inconvenienced for the sake of the Gospel. You are my LORD and KING.

Please continue to show your plans to me. I want to follow you all of my life.

O, Jesus, I offer a special prayer for all the babies who will be murdered this year. I pray for their mothers to choose life, not death for the babies in their wombs.

 If there is one person, who I can lead to you, please guide me. Use me in ways I never thought possible.

I offer you all my praise and worship.

Now, I pray for the following people…

The Massacre of the Holy Innocents[120]
by Domenico Ghirlandaio, 1486- 1490
United States Public Domain

10

The Holy Family Returns from Egypt
The Boy Jesus Teaches the Temple Leaders

Connection Question

Have you ever had a meaningful dream?

The Flight into Egypt[121]
by Bartolomé Esteban Murillo, 1647 – 1650 AD
United States Public Domain

Chapter Ten – The Holy Family Returns from Egypt
The Boy Jesus Teaches the Temple Leaders

Twelve Months in Egypt

The journey of the Holy Family from Israel to Egypt--through the desert of shifting sand and scorching heat with little food or water, took at least a week to complete. Mary, Joseph and Baby Jesus must have been exhausted. Although Matthew does not indicate how long the Holy Family stayed in Egypt, history offers an answer. It probably was only 12 months or less, as historically Herod's death was recorded shortly after his execution of the innocents.[122]

Is it any wonder that such evil intended against the Son of God overcame Herod and killed him? Soon Joseph learned in a dream that the evil ruler had died, and he could bring his family back home.

It should be noted that some scholars believe evidence suggests Herod died around 1 BC and Jesus was born about 3 BC [123]. Other scholars believe Herod died around 4 BC and thus, Jesus was born in 6 BC. [124]

You may wonder why Jesus was born in a calendar year labeled BC ("Before Christ") and not in the year labeled AD (*Anno Domini,* Latin for "in the year of our Lord"). According to Fr. Raymond E. Brown, S.S., the BC date results from an ancient mistake in calculating the year of Christ's birth.[125] He says, in 533 AD, Catholic theologian Dionysisu Exiguss proposed our present calendar system. He reckoned the years "no longer from the foundation of Rome (abbreviated A.U.C.), but from the birth of the Lord. He chose 754 A.U.C. as ONE AD — a date too late since Herod died in 750 A.U.C."[126]

Thus, the choice of 1 AD as the date for the birth of Christ was miscalculated and set about four years too late since Herod had died four years previously.

Chapter Ten Questions

1. _WARNED IN A DREAM._ (a) Read Matthew 2: 19-23 and **circle** all the events related to the Holy Family's return to Nazareth. (b) List all the places where the Holy Family traveled or lived.

_____
_____
_____
_____
_____
_____
_____

Matthew 2: 19-23

[19] When Herod died, an angel of the Lord suddenly appeared in a dream to Joseph in Egypt and said, [20] "Get up, take the child and his mother, and go to the land of Israel, for those who were seeking the child's life are dead." [21] Then Joseph got up, took the child and his mother, and went to the land of Israel. [22] But when he heard that Archelaus was ruling over Judea in place of his father Herod, he was afraid to go there. And after being warned in a dream, he went away to the district of Galilee. [23] There he made his home in a town called Nazareth, so that what had been spoken through the prophets might be fulfilled, "He will be called a Nazorean."

2. _CALLED A NAZOREAN._ (a) How did the Holy Family know when to return to Israel? (b) Read John 1: 46 and explain the meaning of the Holy Family's return to Nazareth (v. 23-24)?

_____
_____
_____
_____
_____
_____

John 1: 46. Nathanael said to him, "Can anything good come out of Nazareth?" Philip said to him, "Come and see."

"Jesus, the Nazorean"

Jesus of Nazareth is a name beloved by our Lord because it made him "despised and rejected by others" (Isaiah 53: 3). In 1 Corinthians 1:23-24 we read that Jesus of Nazareth is "a stumbling block to Jews and foolishness to Gentiles, but to those who are the called, both Jews and Greeks, Christ the power of God and the wisdom of God."

The Holy Family may have <u>preferred</u> to raise Jesus in David's holy city of <u>Bethlehem,</u> but instead they followed the angel's direction and returned to *Nazareth,* their home town. Obviously, it was God's plan for Jesus to be raised in Nazareth. This was also a sign of God's dealing with the prejudices of people. <u>Being called a Nazorean was a sign of contempt.</u>[127] Isn't it interesting that the insignificant town of Nazareth was NOT known for religion or learning?

Nazareth was a trade village located in the northern corner of Israel, bordering pagan countries and just down the road from a garrison of Roman soldiers. It was despised by the Jews and situated in Galilee, a province where citizens were known for rude, crude speech and a lack of education.[128] Old Testament prophecies (e.g., Isaiah 53: 2-3) said Jesus would be despised, rejected, and treated as an outcast. It was true—the "religious" and "educated" Scribes and Pharisees would never recognize a Nazorean as their coming savior! In John 1: 46 Nathanial said, "Can any good thing come out of Nazareth," possibly referring to the religious insignificance, smallness or prejudice that was associated with Nazareth.

The expression "spoken through the prophets" (Matthew 2: 23) may be Matthew's way of connecting Jesus from Nazareth with certain Old Testament prophecies about the Messiah. For example, in Isaiah 11:1, the prophecy about Immanuel sprouting from the line of David includes the word "bud or shoot" which is "neser" in Hebrew. In Judges 16: 17, a prophecy used the word "Nazarite" ("I have been a Nazirite of God from my mother's womb"). Nazirite in Hebrew means one who is consecrated to God.[129]

3. _IN MY FATHER'S HOUSE._ (a) Read Luke 2: 39-52 and **circle** all the events related to Jesus teaching in the temple. (b) How long was Jesus missing from his parents.

_____

_____

_____

_____

_____

_____

_____

Luke 2: 39-52

And when they had performed everything according to the law of the Lord, they returned into Galilee, to their own city, Nazareth. 40 And the child grew and became strong, filled with wisdom; and the favor of God was upon him. 41 Now his parents went to Jerusalem every year at the feast of the Passover. 42 And when he was twelve years old, they went up according to custom; 43 and when the feast was ended, as they were returning, the boy Jesus stayed behind in Jerusalem. His parents did not know it, 44 but supposing him to be in the company they went a day's journey, and they sought him among their kinsfolk and acquaintances; 45 and when they did not find him, they returned to Jerusalem, seeking him. 46 After three days they found him in the temple, sitting among the teachers, listening to them and asking them questions; 47 and all who heard him were amazed at his understanding and his answers. 48 And when they saw him, they were astonished; and his mother said to him, "Son, why have you treated us so? Behold, your father and I have been looking for you anxiously." 49 And he said to them, "How is it that you sought me? Did you not know that I must be in my Father's house?" 50 And they did not understand the saying which he spoke to them. 51 And he went down with them and came to Nazareth and was obedient to them; and his mother kept all these things in her heart. 52 And Jesus increased in wisdom and in stature, and in favor with God and man. (RSVCE)

Note: The **Feast of the Holy Family** is celebrate on the Sunday following Christmas in the Catholic Church. Luke 2: 41-52 is one of the Mass readings.

4. ***MARY & JOSEPH TAUGHT JESUS.*** (a) Read Deuteronomy 6: 4-9, which explains what Jewish parents were commanded to pass on to their children. (b) List what Mary and Joseph would have taught Jesus through their parenting and by their example. (Keep in mind that Jesus was raised in a Jewish home and trained in the Mosaic Law so that at a young age, he knew the Old Testament scriptures and observed the feast days [e.g., Luke 2:41]). (c) Would these verses apply to you today in any way?

_____

_____

_____

_____

_____

_____

Deuteronomy 6: 4-9. Hear, O Israel: The Lord is our God, the Lord alone. [5] You shall love the Lord your God with all your heart, and with all your soul, and with all your might. [6] Keep these words that I am commanding you today in your heart. [7] Recite them to your children and talk about them when you are at home and when you are away, when you lie down and when you rise. [8] Bind them as a sign on your hand, fix them as an emblem on your forehead, [9] and write them on the doorposts of your house and on your gates. (NRSVCE)

The Feasts

Every year Jewish families made at least three pilgrimages to Jerusalem. They would travel in caravans "to appear before the Lord" and worship Him in Jerusalem (Exodus 23: 17, Exodus 34: 23)."[130] The three important pilgrimage feasts [also called festivals] included Passover, Pentecost and Tabernacles.

The Feast of Passover was a one-day commemoration and special meal observed as part of the seven-day *Feast of Unleavened Bread*. It was held annually in March to April on our calendars today. At the time, the families remembered and thanked God for their escape from Egypt and especially the night when God sent the angel to kill the Egyptian firstborns, but the death angel *passed over* the Israelites' homes marked with the blood of a lamb.

The Feast of Pentecost was a one-day feast celebrated on the fiftieth day after the Passover feast. It occurs in May to June on our calendars today and was also known as the *Feast of Weeks* (referring to *seven weeks* plus one day after Passover). At the time, the Israelites commemorated the day the Torah, including the Ten Commandments, was given to Moses at Mt. Sinai plus they offered joyous thanksgiving to God for the first fruits of their harvest.

The Feast of Tabernacles was a seven-day feast celebrated in September to October on our calendars today. It was also called the *Feast of Booths* and included the "Day of Atonement," or *Yom Kippur* in Hebrew. God had provided for the Israelites in their Exodus journey when they camped in booths or tents while traveling from Egypt to the Promised Land of Canaan. Thus, they commemorated the time by building tabernacles (i.e., tents) for their families to live in where they would offer praise and thanksgiving to God alone as a family.

5. *FEASTS.* (a) Review Luke 2: 40-52 and then (b) record in the blanks below what you learn about Jesus and the Feast of Passover.

The name of the feast is_____	v. 41`
The age of Jesus is _____	v. 42
Mary and Joseph started missing Jesus after_____ days	v. 44
When they could not find Him, they _____	v. 45
They searched for Him for _____	v. 46
They found him (where?) _____	v. 46
When they found Him, Jesus was _____ and _____and _____	v. 46
Those listening to Him were _____	v. 47
Mary and Joseph were _____	v. 48
Mary said _____	v. 48
Jesus asked why they were looking for Him and said _____	v. 49
Mary and Joseph did not _____what Jesus spoke to them	v. 50

Passover

Luke 2: 40-50 gives us more important information than we may think at first glance. By law every adult male within 20 miles of Jerusalem had to attend Passover. At the age of 12, a Jewish boy had to take the full commitment of the law upon him. Can you imagine how a sacred feast would fascinate a 12-year-old? In a caravan, the women would start out on the journey first because they traveled more slowly. The men would join them later at the evening camp. That's when the Holy Couple noticed Jesus was missing. Joseph thought Jesus was in the caravan with Mary, and Mary thought He was with Joseph. Three days later they found Him in the temple court.

During the time of Passover, members of the Sanhedrin and leading rabbis met in the temple court to discuss religious and theological questions. "Hearing and asking questions" was a well-known phrase signifying that a Jewish student was learning and participating in discussion with his teachers.[131]

6. _JESUS FOUND._ (a) What do you think Mary and Joseph were feeling as they searched for their lost son? (b) How do you think they felt when they found him? (c) What does Jesus' response to Mary in Luke 2: 49 tell you about Jesus' or the Holy Family's knowledge of His mission? (*"And Jesus said to them, 'How is it that you sought me? Did you not know that I must be in my Father's house'?"*)

_____

_____

_____

_____

_____

_____

Jesus Was Obedient - The Holy Child Becomes a Man

Jesus was true man and true God. As God, He did not grow in anything. He was full and complete. As man, His body grew in a natural way, and His mind grew in wisdom. He probably learned Aramaic, Hebrew and Greek. As a child, He gave us the example of obedience to His parents. As a man, He gave us the example of obedience to God.

In all this, "His mother treasured all these things in her heart" (Luke 2: 52), which signals to us that Luke likely took these words directly from the lips of Mary. We are also reminded here that Mary, *the Handmaid of the Lord* continued to meditate on the Words of God and on the life of Jesus, just as we must do.

7. *EIGHTEEN YEARS LATER.* (a) Luke 2: 51-52 includes all that Luke tells us about the next 18 years of Jesus' life. What do you imagine Jesus did with those 18 years? (*And he went down with them and came to Nazareth and was obedient to them; and his mother kept all these things in her heart.* 52 *And Jesus increased in wisdom and in stature, and in favor with God and man.*")
(b) Describe anything you further learn about Jesus in the v. 51-52.
(c) How do you think He related to His family, other relatives and the neighbors?

_____

_____

_____

_____

_____

_____

8. _HOMETOWN._ (a) What do Matthew 13: 54-58 and Mark 6: 3-4 indicate about the ordinary home life of Jesus? (b) What did the neighbors and relatives say about Jesus when he came into His ministry 18 years later.

_____

_____

_____

_____

_____

_____

_____

_____

Matthew 13:54-58. He came to his hometown and began to teach the people in their synagogue, so that they were astounded and said, "Where did this man get this wisdom and these deeds of power? 55 Is not this the carpenter's son? Is not his mother called Mary? And are not his brothers James and Joseph and Simon and Judas? 56 And are not all his sisters with us? Where then did this man get all this?" 57 And they took offense at him. But Jesus said to them, "Prophets are not without honor except in their own country and in their own house." 58 And he did not do many deeds of power there, because of their unbelief. NRSVCE

Mark 6: 3-4. 3 Is not this the carpenter, the son of Mary and brother of James and Joses and Judas and Simon, and are not his sisters here with us?" And they took offense at him. 4 Then Jesus said to them, "Prophets are not without honor, except in their hometown, and among their own kin, and in their own house." NRSVCE

Note: "Jesus' brothers and sisters" likely referred to his cousins. Jesus was close to his cousins and was raised in an extended family culture. The terms "brothers and sisters" translated from the original Greek of the New Testament are the same words used interchangeably for "cousins."

Jesus Lived an Ordinary Childhood.

Jesus lived an ordinary life. Most Reverend Fulton J. Sheen illuminated this when he said:

"For 18 uneventful years, He lived under a humble roof, obedient to His parents…He fixed the flat roofs of Nazarene homes and mended the wagons of the farmers. Every mean and lowly task was part of the Father's business. Human development of the God-man unfolded in the village so naturally that not even the town people were conscious of the greatness of Him who dwelled in their midst."[132]

St. Justin Martyr also wrote that Jesus made plows and yokes and that He continues to teach us holy and right living with God through the product of His peaceful toil. Thus, the ordinary life of the Son of God should remind us to ask God to help us recognize Jesus in our ordinary daily tasks.

9. REFLECTION ON JESUS. (a) How do you respond to *Jesus, the Nazorean*? (b) Are you willing to be rejected or persecuted for Jesus' name sake, just as he was? (c) In summary of your journey with Jesus in this book, what did you find most joyful in the events, people and prayers related to Jesus' first coming?

_____

_____

_____

_____

_____

_____

_____

_____

_____

_____

_____

10. _MY PERSONAL PRAYER RESPONSE_. Please write a prayer to Jesus based on what this book and study has meant to you. See the following example.

_____
_____
_____
_____
_____
_____
_____
_____
_____
_____
_____
_____
_____
_____
_____
_____
_____
_____
_____
_____
_____

PRAYER EXAMPLE

Dear Jesus, I praise you.

Thank you for coming as the Nazorean.

Thank you for suffering, dying and paying the price for my sins. You were despised and rejected for me.

I give you my life and take you as My Lord and Savior.

O Lord, strengthen me so that I can endure the rejections and persecutions that I receive for knowing you and standing up for you.

I want to be willing to be despised and rejected for you, as you were for me.

Help me to come along side those who are suffering for you.

Lord, I pray that by your grace, I might teach the children in my life the habits of worship that will stay with them forever.

Today, I offer to you all the ordinary tasks in my life. Please sanctify them and receive them as an offering to you.

Fill me with the joy of knowing you.

Jesus, I love you. Jesus, I praise you. Jesus, you are the Joy of my Life.

I confess my faith with the Apostles Creed:

I believe in God,
the Father almighty,
Creator of heaven and earth,
and in Jesus Christ, his only Son, our Lord,
who was conceived by the Holy Spirit,
born of the Virgin Mary,
suffered under Pontius Pilate,
was crucified, died and was buried.
He descended into hell.
On the third day he rose again from the dead.
He ascended into heaven,
and is seated at the right hand of God the Father almighty.
From there he will come to judge the living and the dead.

I believe in the Holy Spirit,
the Holy Catholic Church,
the communion of saints,
the forgiveness of sins,
the resurrection of the body,
and life everlasting.
Amen

Appendix

The Holy Family with a Bird[133]
by Bartolomé Esteban Murillo, 1618 – 1682
United States Public Domain

Tips for Small Groups

This Bible study is designed for use as a journal for personal reflection, for RCIA programs, high school religion classes or small group study.

Preparation

In preparation for sharing as part of a group discussion, please try to follow these basic guidelines:

1. Prepare in advance by completing the chapter for each session.
2. Come to each session ready to contribute to the discussion.
3. Keep the focus on the study questions and commentary; avoid discussions on side issues or current events that can distract the group from focusing on God's Word.
4. Pray daily for the members of your group.

Tips for Facilitating Small Group Study

Each small group needs a facilitator who can foster discussion and keep the group focused on the questions and commentary. A facilitator should:

Welcome. Welcome each of the participants.

Review. Go over the basic guidelines for small groups (see previous page).

Pray. Begin each meeting with thanksgiving and prayer, especially invoking the Holy Spirit to guide the session. For example, you could pray the *Come Holy Spirit Prayer* (see the end of this section for the prayer).

Read. Begin by asking someone to read the commentary at the beginning of the chapter. (This study is designed so that each chapter is self-contained and thus, all the information needed for each session is provided in the chapter.) Plan to go through an entire chapter together as a group.

Invite. When you get to each study question, as the facilitator, read each question aloud and pause so that group members have time to share their answers to each question.

Involve. Try to maintain involvement by inviting each member to read a Scripture reading or a commentary section.

Encourage all to participate in the discussion so that no one person monopolizes the session or feels left out.

Focus. Keep the focus on each question and do not allow the group to be distracted from the questions and commentary. If someone tries to lead the group astray on a subject unrelated to a question, simply say, "We can discuss that later—after the meeting, but for now let's stay focused on the question and the Scriptures."

Commentary. Emphasize the commentary, word studies and notes. This study contains supplementary information from historical sources, Catholic Scholars and the Catechism of the Catholic Church.

Follow-up. Encourage each group member to do the chapter study and answer the questions before coming to the session. It will have a huge impact on the depth of the discussion if everyone has prepared in advance. You might also suggest they pray with the chapter after the meeting, and thus, allow the Lord to lead them more deeply into the Word of God.

Prayer. End each session with prayer. You might choose to invite *popcorn prayer** where each person prays a one-sentence prayer for personal needs and then says, "For this I pray to the Lord." Everyone responds, "Lord, hear our prayer." You can go around the room so that everyone can share their one-sentence prayer.

---

*Note. Popcorn prayer is defined as a type of corporate prayer where individuals verbalize their prayers in random order—it resembles popcorn popping as each one expresses one or two words, phrases, or sentences of praise or petition and as the small group facilitator directs. For thanksgivings, the responsorial is: "For this we Praise and Thank You Lord Jesus." "For petitions, after the short request, the person says: "For this I pray to the Lord" and those present respond, "Lord, Hear Our Prayer."

The use of popcorn prayer is based on Jesus' words in Matthew 18:19, "Truly I tell you, if two of you agree on earth about anything you ask, it will be done for you by my Father in heaven." In a small group, it is important to keep petitions short and allow everyone to prayerfully focus and agree about each petition. Jesus reminds us in Matthew 6:7 that we should not think God hears us more when we use many words. Instead, He hears our hearts and He knows our needs.

Final Tip for New Facilitators. If you want to start a new study group, ask the Lord for his counsel—who you should invite to the group, and if there is someone who could help you get a small group study started. Then the two of you will want to pray together often for each other and for the group members. Remember, Jesus sent the disciples out to minister two-by-two. (Luke 9: 1-6)

The Come Holy Spirit Prayer

Come Holy Spirit,
fill the hearts of your faithful
and kindle in them the fire of your love.
Send forth your Spirit
and they shall be created.
And You shall renew the face of the earth.

O, God, who by the light of the Holy Spirit,
did instruct the hearts of the faithful,
grant that by the same Holy Spirit
we may be truly wise
and
ever enjoy His consolations,
Through Christ Our Lord. Amen.

Reference List

Baker, D. Editor (1994). The Complete Word Study Old Testament. Chattanooga, TN: AMG Publishers.

Barclay, W. (1956). Gospel of Luke. Philadelphia: Westminster Press.

Barclay, W. (1950). Gospel of Matthew. Philadelphia: Westminster Press.

Benedict XVI (2012). Jesus of Nazareth: The Infancy Narratives. New York Image.

Brown, Rev. Raymond E., S.S. (1993, 1977). The Birth of the Messiah: A Commentary on the Infancy Narratives in the Gospels of Matthew and Luke. New York: Doubleday.

Brook, J. (1992). School of Prayer. Collegeville, MN: Liturgical Press.

Catechism of the Catholic Church (CCC, 1993). Libreria Editrice Vaticana, Citta del Vaticano 1993.
http://www.vatican.va/archive/ENG0015/_INDEX.HTM#fonte

Drum, W. (1912). Zacharias. In The Catholic Encyclopedia. New York: Robert Appleton Company. Retrieved August 2, 2017 from New Advent: http://www.newadvent.org/ cathen/15741b.htm

Eisenberg, R. L. (2004, 2008). The JPS Guide to Jewish Traditions. Philadelphia: The Jewish Publication Society.

Fernandez, Rev. Francis (1997). Conversation with God, vol. 1. London: Scepter.

Goodier, Most Rev. Alban, S. J. (1982). The Prince of Peace. Boston: The Daughters of St. Paul.

Hahn, S. (2014). Joy to the World. New York, Image.

Hahn, S., & Mitch, C. (2001a). Commentary. The Ignatius Catholic Study Bible, The Gospel of Matthew. San Francisco: Ignatius Press.

Hahn, S., & Mitch, C. (2001b). Commentary. The Ignatius Catholic Study Bible, The Gospel of Luke. San Francisco: Ignatius Press.

Hardon, Rev. John A, S. J. (2001). Modern Catholic Dictionary. Bardstown, KY:
    Eternal Life.

John Paul II (2004). Psalms and Canticles: Meditations and Catechesis on Psalms
and Canticles of Morning Prayer. Chicago: Liturgy Training Publications.

John Paul II (1981). Familiaris Consortio, 22 November 1981.

Josephus, Flavius, (1987). The Works of Josephus. (W. Whiston Trans.) Peabody,
    MA: Hendrickson Publishers.

Knecht, Most Reverend F. J., (1923, 2003). A Practical Commentary on Holy
Scripture. Rockford, Il; Tan Books and Publishers, Inc.

Liturgy of the Hours (1975). New York: Catholic Book Publishing Company.

Longenecker, D. (2017). Mystery of the Magi. Washington DC: Regnery History.

Merriam-Webster's Collegiate Dictionary, 11th ed., (2003). Springfield, MA:
Merriam-Webster.

The Navarre Bible Saint Luke: Texts and Commentaries (1988). Dublin: Four
Courts Press.

The Navarre Bible Saint Matthew: Texts and Commentaries (1988). Dublin: Four
Courts Press.

New American Bible and Notes (NAB Notes), St. Joseph Edition, 1970.

Pius IX (1958). Ineffabilis Deus, 8 December 1954.

Paul VI. (1968). Creed of the People of God, 30 June 1968.

Prat, Fr. Ferdinand, S. J. (1950). Jesus Christ: His Life, His Teaching, and His
Work.   Milwaukee: Bruce Publishing. (John J. Heenan, S. J., Trans.)

Ricciotti, Abbott Fr. Gieuseppe (1947). The Life of Christ. Milwaukee: Bruce
Publishing.

Scotto, Fr. D. F. (1987). Liturgy of the Hours. New York: Catholic Book
Publishing.

Sheen, Most Reverend F. J. (1958). Life of Christ. New York: McGraw-Hill.

St. Augustine. Sermo de Nativitate Domini, in Toal.

St. Leo, I, the Great (1954). Dogmatic Epistle 28, the Incarnation (The Sources of Catholic Dogma, Fitzwilliam, NH: Loreto Publications.

St. Bernard. Sermons on the Canticles in Toal.

St. Josemaria Escriva (1973). Christ Is Passing By. London: Scepter Publishers.

Souvay, C. (1907). Baal, Baalim. In The Catholic Encyclopedia. New York: Robert Appleton Company. Retrieved August 2, 2017 from New Advent http:// www.newadvent.org /cathen/02175a.htm

Tierney, J. (1910). Herod. In The Catholic Encyclopedia. New York: Robert Appleton Company. Retrieved August 2, 2017 from New Advent: http://www.newadvent.org/cathen/07289c.htm

Thurston, H. J., & Attwater, D. (1981). Butler's Lives of the Saints. Westminster, MD: Christian Classics, Inc.

Toal, D.D. (2000). The Sunday Sermons of the Great Fathers. San Francisco, Ignatius Press.

Vatican Council II. Gaudium et Spes.

Vatican Council II. Lumen Gentium.

Walsh, Msgr. V. (1980). Lead My People. Holland, PA: Key of David Publications.

Whyte, A. (1990, 1986). Bible Characters from the Old and New Testaments. Grand Rapids, MI: Kregel Publications.

Willis, J. (2002). The Teachings of the Church Fathers. San Francisco: Ignatius Press.

Zodhiates, S. (1992). The Complete Word Study Dictionary New Testament. Chattanooga, TN: AMG Publishers.

Endnotes

---

[1] https://upload.wikimedia.org/wikipedia/commons/2/2a/Correggio_-_The_Holy_Night_-_Google_Art_Project.jpg

[2] https://commons.wikimedia.org/wiki/File%3AAngel_Appearing_to_Zacharias

[3] Merriam Webster. http://www.merriamwebster.com/dictionary/annunciation; Dictionary.com. http://www.dictionary.com/browse/annunciation,

[4] Abbott Fr. Gieuseppe Ricciotti, 1947

[5] Drum, Catholic Encyclopedia- Zacharias, http://www.newadvent.org/cathen/15741b.htm

[6] Pope Benedict, Http://W2.Vatican.Va/Content/BenedictXvi/En/Audiences/2011/ Documents /Hf_Ben-Xvi_Aud_20111130.Html, Benedict Xvi, General Audience, Paul Vi Audience Hall, Wednesday, 30 November 2011

[7] Fr. Raymond Brown, 1993

[8] Abbott Fr. Gieuseppe Ricciotti, 1947

[9] Fr. Raymond Brown, 1993

[10] Fr. John Hardon, S. J., 2001

[11] Navarre Bible Commentary, St Luke, p. 34

[12] Fr. Ferdinand Pratt, S. J., 1950

[13] St. John Paul II (1981). Familiaris Consortio, November 22, 1981

[14] Souvay, 1910, The Catholic Encyclopedia – Zacharias.

[15] Bible Characters from the Old and New Testaments, Kregel Publications, Grand Rapids, MI, p. 459-461

[16] https://commons.wikimedia.org/wiki/File%3ADomenico_Beccafumi_-_The_Annunciation_-_WGA01551.jpg

[17] Fr. John Hardon, S. J., 2001

[18] Abbott Fr. Gieuseppe Ricciotti, 1947

[19] Baker, 1994; Fr. Raymond Brown, 1993; Abbott Fr. Gieuseppe Ricciotti, 194

[20] St. Augustine in Willis, 2002

[21] Catechism of the Catholic Church (CCC) #430; #432, Acts 4:12

[22] Most Reverend Fulton Sheen, 1958, p.19

[23] St Augustine. Letters, No. 1 37 ML 33, 519, RCXX, 24, in John Willis, 2002

[24] CCC #495

[25] Vatican II, Lumen Gentium, 50

[26] Most Rev. Alban Goodier, S.J., 1982, p. 49

[27] St. Josemaria Escriva, p. 174

[28] https://commons.wikimedia.org/wiki/File%3AChampaigne_visitation.jpg

[29] St Ambrose, A Commentary on Luke, Lib. 2. p. 22-23

[30] Merriam Webster Dictionary, 2011

[31] Most Rev. Alban Goodier, S.J., 1982, p. 55

[32] Barclay, Gospel of Luke, 1956, p. 9-10

[33] Brock, 1992, p. 117

[34] Vines; Zodhiates #21

[35] CCC #2097

[36] Fr. Fernandez, 1997, p. 112

[37] https://commons.wikimedia.org/wiki/File:Jacopo_Pontormo_031.jpg

[38] Navarre Bible Commentary, St Luke, 1988, p. 47

[39] Eisenberg, 2004

[40] Eisenberg, 2004

[41] CCC #1267

[42] CCC #1279

[43] CCC #1280

[44] St. Ambrose in Willis, 2002

[45] Brook, 1992

[46] Merriam Webster's Collegiate Dictionary

[47] Thurston and Attwater, 1981, p. 632

[48] Brock, 1992, p. 144

[49] John Paul II, 2004, p. 283

[50] Abbott Fr. Gieuseppe Ricciotti, 1947, p. 233

[51] https://commons.wikimedia.org/wiki/File:Anton_Raphael_Mengs_016.jpg

[52] Pope Emeritus Benedict XVI, 2012, Jesus of Nazareth: The Infancy Narratives

[53] Pope Emeritus Benedict XVI, 2012, p. 8

[54] Pope Emeritus Benedict XVI, 2012, p. 6

[55] Pope Emeritus Benedict XVI, 2012, p. 10

[56] Hahn, 2014

[57] Navarre Bible Commentary, St. Matthew, 1950, p. 28

[58] Pope Emeritus Benedict XVI, 2012, p. 12-13

[59] Abbott Fr. Gieuseppe Ricciotti, 1947, p. 234-235

[60] Fr. Raymond Brown, 1997

[61] Fr. Fernandez, 1997, p. 162

[62] Abbott Fr. Gieuseppe Ricciotti, 1947, p. 235-236

[63]https://commons.wikimedia.org/wiki/File:Domenichino_(Domenico_Zampieri),_The_Adoration_of_the_Shepherds,_c._1607-10,_Oil_on_canvas,_143_x_115cm,_National_Gallery_of_Scotland.jpg

[64] https://commons.wikimedia.org/wiki/File%3ADomenichino_ (Domenico_Zampieri) %2C_The_Adoration_of_the_Shepherds%2C_c._1607-10%2C_Oil_on_canvas%2C_143_x_115cm%2C_National_Gallery_of_Scotland.jpg

[65] Abbott Fr. Gieuseppe Ricciotti, 1947

[66] Most Reverend Fulton J. Sheen, 1958

[67] Abbott Fr. Gieuseppe Ricciotti, 1947

[68] Helvidium, 10; Navarre Bible Commentary, St Matthew

[69] http://catholicism.org/what-are-swaddling-clothes-and-what-is-their-significance.html

[70] Most Reverend Fulton J. Sheen, 1958, p.13

[71] Most Reverend Fulton J. Sheen, 1958, p.4

[72] Navarre Bible Commentary, St Matthew, p. 52

[73] Zodhiates' #4592

[74] CCC #333

[75] St. Gregory the Great, Moralia, 28, 7 in Navarre Bible Commentary, St Luke, 1988, p. 54

[76] CCC #430

[77] CCC #430

78 CCC #446

79 CCC #449

80 Fr. Ferdinand Pratt, S. J., 1950

81 https://commons.wikimedia.org/wiki/File%3ABrooklyn_Museum_-_The_Presentation_of_Jesus_in_the_Temple_(La_pr%C3%A9sentation_de_J%C3%A9sus_au_Temple)_-_James_Tissot_-_overall.jpg

82 CCC #2666

83 CCC #452

84 Second Vatican Council, *Gaudium et spes*, 45

85 Fr. Fernandez, 1997, p. 299-300

86 St. John Paul, p. 15

87 Most Reverend Fulton J. Sheen, 1957, p. 27

88 https://commons.wikimedia.org/wiki/File%3APhilippe_de_Champaigne_The_Presentation_of_the_Temple.jpg

89 Abbott Fr. Gieuseppe Ricciotti,1947

90 Navarre Bible Notes, Luke, p. 59

91 Most Rev. Alban Goodier, S.J., 1982, p. 104

92 Msgr. Vincent Walsh, 1980

93 Most Rev. Alban Goodier, S.J., *1982,* p, 111

94 CCC #682, $1039

95 Text by Jan Struther-1901, Melody: Allons, Suivons, Les Mages 76.76.676

96 https://commons.wikimedia.org/wiki/File%3AJames_Tissot_-_Journey_of_the_Magi_-_70.21_-_Minneapolis_Institute_of_Arts.jpg

97 CCC #528

[98] Stromata 1 15, http://www.newadvent.org/fathers/02101.htm

[99] Fr. Dwight Longenecker, 2017

[100] Fr. Longenecker, 2017

[101] Fr. Ferdinand Pratt, S. J., 1950

[102] Fr. Raymond Brown, p. 1993

[103] St. Leo the Great, Thurston & Attwater, 1981

[104] McKenzie, J. L., S. J.

[105] St. Augustine, Sermon 2, et 7, de Epiph in Willis, 2002

[106] CCC #528

[107] Fr. Raymond Brown, Fr. Ferdinand Pratt, S. J., 1950

[108] Fr. Ferdinand Pratt, S. J., 1950

[109] Knecht, Most Reverend F. J., 2003

[110] St. Irenaeus, Against the Heretics III ix 2 in Brown, 1993

[111] St. Gregory, PL 74, 1110, hom 10 on the Gospels in Toal, D.D., 2000

[112] Fr. Mark McKercher, St. Robert Bellarmine Church, Omaha, 1-4-2021.

[113] Longenecker, 2017

[114] Fr. Raymond Brown, 1993

[115] St. John Chrysostom, PL 7, 81, sermo 8 in Toal, D.D., 2000

[116] Fr. Raymond Brown, Thurston & Attwater, 1981

[117] Fr. Ferdinand Pratt, S. J., 1950

[118] Thurston & Attwater, 1981, p. 626

[119] Barclay, 1950

[120]https://commons.wikimedia.org/wiki/File%3ACappella_Tornabuoni%2C_
Slaughter_of_the_Innocents_01.jpg

[121] https://commons.wikimedia.org/wiki/File%3ABartolome_murillo-
huida_egipto.jpg

[122] Fr. Raymond Brown, 1993, Fr. Ferdinand Pratt, S. J., 1950

[123] e.g., Hahn and Mitch, 2001a

[124] e.g., Fr. Raymond Brown, 1993

[125] Fr. Raymond Brown, 1993

[126] Fr. Raymond Brown, 1993, p. 167

[127] Most Rev. Alban Goodier, S.J., 1982

[128] Most Reverend Fulton Sheen, 1958

[129] Fr. Raymond Brown, 1993

[130] Fr. Raymond Brown, 1993, p. 472

[131] Barclay, The Gospel of Luke, 1956

[132] Most Reverend Fulton J. Sheen, 1958

[133] https://commons.wikimedia.org/wiki/File%3ASagrada_Familia_del_pajarito_
(Murillo) jpg

www.ingramcontent.com/pod-product-compliance
Lightning Source LLC
Chambersburg PA
CBHW052330100426
42737CB00055B/3299